Today's Kindergarten

EXPLORING THE KNOWLEDGE BASE, EXPANDING THE CURRICULUM

Edited by
Bernard Spodek

Teachers College, Columbia University
New York and London

Published by Teachers College Press, 1234 Amsterdam Avenue,
New York, N.Y. 10027

Library of Congress Cataloging in Publication Data

Today's kindergarten.
  (Early childhood education series)
  Bibliography: p.
  Includes index.
  1. Kindergarten — Methods and manuals.
I. Spodek, Bernard.   II. Series.
LB1169.T63   1986   372'.218   86-5712

ISBN 0-8077-2809-8
ISBN 0-8077-2808-X (pbk.)

Manufactured in the United States of America

91 90 89 88 87   2 3 4 5 6

Contents

Contents

Introduction

Tremendous changes have taken place in American kindergarten education over the past two decades. Probably the most striking change has been increased attendance and the almost universal availability of kindergarten within the public schools. In 1965, for example, only about 47% of 5-year-olds were enrolled in kindergarten. Today that figure is about 90%, and about 88% of those children are enrolled in public schools. All states today support kindergarten as part of the public elementary schools. Considering the fact that in the vast majority of states kindergarten attendance is not compulsory, this high level of enrollment is evidence of the faith that American families have in the value of kindergarten education.

Some of the same influences that have caused kindergarten enrollments to increase dramatically have led educators and others to suggest that there is a need to modify the kindergarten program. Kindergarten was once seen as the young child's introduction to education outside the home. Attending kindergarten served to ease the transition from home to school. Today, however, most kindergarten teachers find that more than half of the children entering their classes have already had some previous early childhood education experience. Some have been enrolled in nursery school, while others have been enrolled in Montessori schools. Many have been enrolled in all-day child care programs, often for as long as 2 years or more, prior to kindergarten admission.

Some educators have argued that, since most of the children in kindergarten already have had 1 or even 2 years of prior education, kindergarten programs ought to be modified to take this learning into consideration. Kindergartens could become more educationally advanced. What has been taught in the primary grades might now be taught in kindergarten. Others argue that whatever the prior educational experience, kindergarten children as 5-year-olds are not any more mature than they ever have been and that traditional kindergarten programs, which have always served 5-year-olds well, will continue to do so. Still others take the view that while prior education ought to make a difference in what kind of education is offered to children at kindergarten age, there are no quality controls on prekindergarten experiences and thus no way of determining what or how much children have learned in educational programs before kindergarten. They cite evidence that many of the personnel in child care centers have minimal educational preparation. Some of these caregivers have taken only two or three child-related courses beyond high school, and some have had even less teacher preparation than that.

In addition to earlier school experiences, other changes in children's experiences and in the social context of those experiences have also led to suggestions that kindergarten programs need to be modified. Children are viewed as more verbal and more knowledgeable today than they were in the past. They have been offered a great deal of information through television, travel, and better forms of communication. They have contact with computers, use the telephone, and watch films. These differences between children in the past and children today suggest their increased educability.

The social environment in which children are being reared today is also different from that of previous generations. Families have been getting smaller; fewer children are being raised in each family unit. There has been an increase in the proportion of single-parent families and an increase in the proportion of families in which both parents, or the lone parent, work. There have been more teenage pregnancies, with teenage mothers giving birth to and raising their children.

There has also been increasing evidence that early education makes a significant and long-lasting difference in the education and lives of children, especially those who have the highest educational risk. Evidence from programs for handicapped children and programs for low income children suggests that the positive educational effects of preprimary programs can be identified well into high school and beyond.

All these influences together have stimulated the development of new and augmented kindergarten programs. States that have not offered kindergarten in the past are supporting universal kindergarten education in the public schools. In states where kindergartens are already a part of the public schools, there is support for providing all-day every-day kindergarten programs as well as extending kindergarten education to 4-year-olds. The all-day kindergarten, it should be noted, is an all-school-day program, shorter by many hours than the extended day of the child care center. Such programs do not themselves meet the need for child care services for children of working parents, although in some communities extended-school-day programs have also been developed for young children.

The present expansion of kindergarten programs provides a wonderful opportunity for early childhood educators to improve educational services for young children. It has also been seen, however, as cause for alarm.

Just as there is the potential for increasing the good that is done for children as a result of this expansion, there is the possibility that poor educational programs might exploit children and cause harm. So great is the concern today that a number of national, state, regional, and local associations concerned with the education of young children have issued position papers in an attempt to influence the direction of the change that is taking place in kindergartens today. These papers usually represent statements of value or belief about what is good for children. Such value statements are important, but they are not an adequate basis for developing new program proposals or for testing the validity of proposed programs. Other knowledge is required.

This volume explores the areas of knowledge that need to be addressed in formulating a policy related to kindergarten education. While this book is not exhaustive, it does discuss the most critical areas of concern. It is addressed to all professionals making critical decisions on the education of young children, all leaders of early childhood programs, some beginning early childhood or child development students, and most advanced students in early childhood education or child development. The material in this book can also be meaningful to in-service teachers.

Herbert Zimiles, in his chapter "The Social Context of Early Childhood in an Era of Expanding Preschool Education," examines the changing nature of childhood in contemporary society and its implications for early education. With the changing outlook of families, he writes, "educators are being called upon to take up the slack of diminished family care and commitment . . . [while] they are accorded less respect." He also speculates about whether children will later show adverse effects from the current pressure to accelerate academically. Possibly most important, Zimiles paints a picture of today's young children as verbal, poised, and assertive, as having many of the positive traits that would suggest increased educability while at the same time lacking some of the elements that teachers take for granted. A mixed picture of young children is presented that suggests we may need to study in greater depth the effects of earlier schooling and of earlier separation of young children from their families. We will need to develop educational approaches that come to grips with the changing responsiveness of children to school. It may very well be that teachers will need to help children develop alternative cognitive styles as they adapt traditional instructional strategies.

In his chapter "Bilingual Development and the Education of Bilingual Children During Early Childhood," Eugene E. García focuses on a part of the child population that is expanding today. The research evidence on bilingualism and bilingual education is far more unequivocal. While it is evident that bilingual programs do not retard the language or cognitive development of the children they enroll, research needs to continue exploring their potential positive effects. Given the significance of the early years for language development, the kindergarten will continue to play an important role in the education of bilingual children.

As we look at early childhood programs over the years, we can see the many purposes served by these programs and how the content of these programs at each historical period has been related to different conceptions of knowledge. In my chapter "Development, Values, and Knowledge in the Kindergarten Curriculum," I demonstrate how each early childhood program has reflected a view of the nature of knowledge at a particular point in time. The call to bring the education of young children "back to basics" actually suggests that an earlier conception of knowledge is adequate to enable children to understand the contemporary world. Limiting early childhood programs to teaching literacy, however, makes sense only when knowledge is rooted in the authority of a book. When children must learn to deal with different forms of knowledge and must ultimately be responsible for discovering and creating new knowledge, this approach is inadequate. It is self-defeating for a dynamic industrial society, though it might have made sense for Americans in earlier centuries.

The succeeding chapters concern themselves with the content of kindergarten learning. Certainly the most controversial issue in kindergarten education today is the place of reading in the kindergarten curriculum. Jana M. Mason, in "Kindergarten Reading: A Proposal for a Problem-Solving Approach," suggests that there are a number of outmoded notions about how children learn to read, write, and listen. She proposes an approach to beginning reading instruction in the kindergarten that utilizes problem solving. It requires a literacy-rich and supportive environment, a multifaceted program that extends beyond reading and copying material and emphasizes active learning. This approach grows out of contemporary research related to literacy and language development in young children.

Constance Kamii, in her review "Cognitive Learning and Development," builds upon the work of Jean Piaget to suggest what can be learned by kindergarten children in relation to science and mathematics and how they can learn this. Since children construct knowledge by "putting things into relationships through their own mental activity," they need to be provided with kindergarten activities that allow them to be mentally active. Various experiments and games can be offered that allow children to think about what is happening independently of the teacher. The child's intellectual autonomy, necessary for him to be a constructor of knowledge, requires that programs of science and mathematics go beyond telling and showing and allow for each child's personal exploration of the physical world and the world of quantity.

One way in which children explore the world is through play activities. Such activities have been considered an important part of early childhood education since the creation of the original kindergarten. Olivia N. Saracho, in her chapter, "Play and Young Children's Learning," reviews the literature related to the cognitive, creative, language, social, and physical elements of play. This review asserts the value of play in kindergarten. It suggests that positive educational outcomes do not result naturally from play. Teachers must have an active role in establishing educational play situations, in guiding educational play, and in appropriately intervening in children's play.

Social learning has always been a focus of kindergarten education. Shirley G. Moore's chapter "Socialization in the Kindergarten Classroom" draws together a wide range of knowledge related to helping establish prosocial behavior in kindergarten children. She discusses helping children to have friendly interactions with others and to show consideration for others, as well as developing school responsibility, which includes developing compliance with authority, achievement behavior, and predispositions to work cooperatively with others. Kindergarten continues to be a place where significant social learning takes place. The social knowledge gained by children at this level serves them as they move throughout the grades.

The knowledge reviewed in this volume can help teachers and policymakers reassess today's kindergarten curriculum. Some elements of kindergarten programs that have been with us for generations continue to be supported as worthwhile educational activities. Other elements, however, might be discarded or modified. Each judgment must be made in relation to what we know about young children today, what we know about the consequences of what we do with children, and about what we consider to be valuable and socially relevant knowledge for children growing up today in America.

Bernard Spodek

CHAPTER 1

The Social Context
of Early Childhood in an Era
# of Expanding Preschool Education

Herbert Zimiles

During the current era of expanding preschool education, children are growing up amid a whirlwind of change. Therefore, planning the expansion of preschool education must take into account the multiple forces of social and technological change that affect the development of young children, forces that impinge on their family life and their educational experience. This chapter considers the implications of current trends of change in early childhood and family life for the expansion of preschool education. It is based, in part, on the findings of an exploratory study conducted by the author of retrospective observations of how children are changing, how school-age children of today are perceived by experienced teachers and clinicians as different from their counterparts of a generation ago (Zimiles, 1984).

THE CHANGING CHARACTER OF EARLY EDUCATION

Only a few decades ago, early childhood education existed on a comparatively modest scale and was bifurcated; it provided preschool care for 4- and 5-year-olds along two quite different tracks — nursery school and day care. In recent years there has been a blurring of the distinction between these two approaches — a convergence of these two streams of early education — and a downward extension in age coverage that now includes extensive programming for infants as well as for toddlers.

The distinction between nursery school and day care was as sharp as the division in social-class background among the comparatively few families that used these quite different resources. Nursery schools, building upon and implementing the tenets of the body of theory and knowl-

1

edge of the early childhood education movement (Isaacs, 1936; Biber, 1934, 1984), were for the most part reserved for the privileged children of progressive-minded middle-class families who were willing and able to pay tuition costs for preschool education. Such programs were designed to provide a milieu for creative play, intellectual exploration, and social intercourse aimed at enriching children's development while at the same time easing their transition to universal public schooling.

Day care, on the other hand, while serving children of the same age during the course of a much longer school day, was organized and staffed to be more custodial. Children in day care almost invariably came from underprivileged homes in which the mother had no choice but to go to work or was unable for other reasons to provide adequate care for her children. Thus, children attended day care out of necessity, while privileged children attended nursery school for their edification and to provide mothers with a measure of relief from the rigors of child care. Children who attended day care remained there for the entire day, a period of time that was then deemed to be much longer than desirable for a young child to be away from home. Day care ministered to children's physical needs for food, rest, and protection. In effect, nursery schools were educational programs for privileged children, and day care was a form of substitutive child care provided for underprivileged children. There were in many cases a sizable overlap in the programs for children under these quite different auspices of early childhood education, but the differences between the programs and the families from which the children came usually outweighed their similarities.

The federally sponsored "war on poverty" of the 1960s, especially the launching of Project Head Start and the expansion of day care (Zigler & Valentine, 1979), served to increase markedly the early education facilities available to families of the poor. This expansion formed a bridge between the private nursery schools for the middle class and the day care centers for the poor. In urging heavy investment in education programs for very young children, child development specialists and educators pointed to the formative influences of the early years and the importance of establishing a sound foundation that could better support the educational edifice still to be built. However, at the same time that Project Head Start was being advocated as a mechanism for supporting the developmental and educational needs of all children and thereby extending the child-centered ethos of nursery school education to programs for children who were not economically privileged, it was recognized that the developmental needs of poor children ranged far beyond those that could be met by means of educational stimulation alone. Underprivileged children and their families also needed improved nutrition, medical care, social services, and access to other community resources usually not available to them. Early childhood programs that were exclusively concerned with delivering services to children during the school day but left untouched the economic and social privations of their families seemed destined for failure. Not only was Head Start designed to provide social services and medical and nutritional services to the families of children of the poor; early education programs were also seen as vehicles for guiding parents to become more actively involved in their children's education. Further, these educational programs became settings that would provide gainful employment for the families of the children who were being served.

Thus Project Head Start helped to bring about two important reassessments of the role of preschool education: By making preschool education available to the poor it helped to transform the public image of early education from that of a luxurious frill for privileged children to that of a commodity needed for all children; it underlined the universal value of preschool education. In addition, Head Start helped to demonstrate that early education programs were capable of solving family, societal, and economic problems as well as delivering educational programs that nourished the psyches of young children; early education programs became instrumentalities for social action (Zimiles, 1985).

THE CHANGING OUTLOOK OF MOTHERS

At the same time that Project Head Start was helping to carry out the mission of the civil rights movement, there were major social changes on other fronts as well. The women's movement led many women to reevaluate their roles and their status both in relation to their families and to the larger society as well. Further, technological advances reduced the burden of housework and made it less necessary for women to stay home in order to "make a home" for their families. For a variety of reasons, many mothers have become more career-minded and work-oriented. Those women who are well educated have become more interested in building a career in their chosen fields and are reluctant to stay home for many years until their children "no longer need them." Those not already professionally trained have also decided to take full-time jobs or have taken advantage of increasing opportunities for continuing education and vocational development. The recent economic decline, which has brought with it inflation and widespread unemployment, has made it necessary for many women to go to work.

The Diminished Presence of Parents

In sharp contrast with the nursery school teacher of yesterday, whose charges came from privileged homes from which they were delivered by dutiful mothers poised to resume their primary caretaking responsibilities after a few hours' respite, the preschool teacher of today deals with children whose parents are largely unavailable to them. Mothers are not available for diverse reasons. Some are committed to full-time careers; they attempt to perform their parenting roles during the confining periods of the evening and weekends. Others must hold full-time jobs because of divorce and, still jolted by the wrench of their family life, are struggling to reshape their own lives. Some must take jobs because their husbands are out of work or because their husbands' incomes are insufficient or at risk. Others are themselves still in adolescence and unmarried. Having decided to forgo an abortion, these teenaged mothers are attempting to find their own way. Other mothers, also unmarried, chose to have children notwithstanding because they were approaching the end of their childbearing period and were intent upon having a child. Other women, married, who postponed having children because they were reluctant to interrupt their work lives, are today freer to face the fact that they are not particularly interested in fully enacting the parent role as it has been traditionally defined. They have decided, instead, to hire other services and other people to fulfill the bulk of their child care responsibilities.

As a result, many children in preschool have families that are for the most part under stress. Either they are struggling with the dual responsibilities of career and parenthood with or without a marital partner, or they are in the throes of divorce, or they are threatened with or are already victimized by unemployment, or they have been plunged into parenthood but are unwilling or unready to face the responsibilities and opportunities of adulthood. These are people who may well want the best for their children and, indeed, may be more aware of the meaning and the importance of psychological well-being and of the value of early learning and of "the beginning" than their forebears. Nevertheless, they are enmeshed in very complicated and taxing life circumstances that leave little time or emotional energy for parenting. In addition, among those intact families who are not subjected to unusually stressful life circumstances, there are many mothers who are distracted by an overstimulating environment that offers unprecedented opportunities for recreation and for supporting personal growth that divert them from the responsibilities of parenting.

In sum, priorities are changing for parents as they experiment with new life styles, explore new modes of resolving conflicts, and encounter new opportunities for gratification and self-fulfillment. At the same time, society has become more open and has shown a greater commitment to alleviating the plight of the underprivileged, especially in those realms in which intervention may forestall even greater and more costly adversity. There is greater tolerance for unconventional and what would have been in previous years regarded as less responsible modes of childbearing and child rearing, and much greater readiness to provide alternative child care and educational resources for those young children whose family structures or economic circumstances appear to be less supportive of child growth and development.

Increasingly, then, educators are being called upon to take up the slack of diminished family care and commitment. There is a curious paradox associated with this shift. As teachers are expected to do more, to expand their roles and responsibilities beyond their traditional definition, they are accorded less respect, as if to minimize, even trivialize, the magnitude of the responsibilities for child care that have been silently transferred from home to school.

New Views of the Power of Early Achievement

In marked contrast to the many parents who are too busy and distracted to support their children's school life, and equally disconcerting to educators, are those who harbor extraordinary ambitions for their very young children. Impressed with the pivotal role of early learning and with the degree to which career patterns appear to evolve from early educational achievements and placements, they are convinced that the path to success begins the moment that children set foot in school. This perspective, often evinced in upwardly mobile communities, leads to strong demands for serious academic instruction and tangible evidence of academic achievement from the very earliest moments of schooling. Teachers are startled and dismayed by these parental expectations of academic progress, which seem inappropriate to the developmental needs of the young child. They believe that the accelerated pace of instruction that many parents are demanding and that some children are actually receiving will deprive children of a much needed time for open and playful exploration, and that these high expectations will impose pressures that will be difficult for many young children to absorb. They speculate that boys, in particular, because of their lagging developmental pace during the early years of elementary school, will show the adverse effects of this premature pressure and acceleration later on.

CHANGING PATTERNS OF CHILD BEHAVIOR
AND CHILDHOOD

In light of the rapid pace of social and technological change, it is not surprising that teachers report seeing changes in children as well as in their families. When compared with their age-mates of a generation ago, kindergarten children are described by teachers as more worldly, as knowing more and having a greater interest in learning. Young children are seen as more advanced in all sectors — whether they be from a working class, rural area or an upwardly mobile suburb where they are frequently spurred to learn to read even before they begin school.

Social Poise and Self-assertiveness

Children are found to be less timid and more assertive and are more comfortable with adults. More verbal and much freer to express themselves, they can barely be restrained from speaking out. Whereas in the past they would seldom interrupt an adult, they now do so as a matter of course. Mainly involved with what they want to say, they hardly listen to each other. It is not simply that they are not interested in what anyone else is saying; many teachers are convinced that they have poor listening skills.

Children seem remarkably sophisticated and self-assured. Their faces, postures, conversations, and overall bearing are those of much older children. The shy young child, commonly observed in the kindergartens of the recent past, is a rarity. A ballet dancer describes children at this age as no longer living in a dream world but in a real world. A first-grade teacher makes the claim: "Children were dull; now they are sharp."

Organization and Discipline

Despite their greater self-assurance, children are seen as less disciplined and less well organized than their counterparts of years back. Coming from households that seem full of motion and turmoil, it is more difficult for them to focus and to concentrate. They show less organization and have learned fewer habits that ritualize elements of self-care and personal management into routines that stamp behaviors into place. For example, when they arrive in school, they are likely to throw their coats on the floor and start right in. When they depart, they tend to forget to take things home with them.

Educability

Although today's children are viewed as knowing more and as being brighter and more alert, it does not necessarily follow that they are easier to teach. Since they are accustomed to greater autonomy, it is more difficult to induce them to conform to the regimen of the classroom or to be responsive to the expectations of the teacher. Most, if not all, have been entertained and stimulated by television from the earliest moments of life. Hence, they have acquired a wide range of information, much of it mystifying but all of it presented entertainingly and in small doses under circumstances that allow the child to regulate what will be watched and for how long. On the one hand, young children, when they arrive in school, know more. On the other hand, they are less likely to regard the school as the eye-opening vehicle that will introduce them to the world beyond their families. They have grown accustomed to learning about the world on their own terms and from sources that use theatrical methods of exposition. It follows, then, that they are more likely to find the mode of the classroom teacher less stimulating and less necessary.

Moreover, it may be speculated that television so heavily exposes children to jumbles of knowledge intermixed with confusion and mystification that they learn to experience less tension in not understanding, and as a result develop less of an expectation to understand something fully and to learn methodically. As a result, children may be less likely to be motivated to learn in school and are less likely to find interest in the instructional transactions of the traditional classroom.

Emotional Stability

Although children are now seen as leading more independent lives and receiving more opportunities to make choices, these changes do not automatically lead to greater emotional maturity. Teachers do not see an acceleration of emotional development that corresponds to their advanced levels of verbal and intellectual development. The egocentricity, level of emotional stability, and characteristic ways of responding to stress by the 5-year-old seem essentially unchanged. In fact, today's young children are more often described as less stable and secure and as more brittle emotionally. They seem to be more panicky, more ready to burst into tears, and more prone to lose their composure. They are also seen as more scrappy.

There appears to be less support for children's emotional development, much less family stability, and less close supervision of young children. Among those young children who have been exposed to extraordinary levels of emotional turbulence and to long periods of neglect, many are seriously impaired in their ability to learn and to relate to others. Clinicians indicate that symptoms of emotional disturbance surface at an earlier age. They report finding many more young children who are disorganized and whose behavior is characterized by impulsivity, low frustration tolerance, demandingness, and problems of modulating expressiveness, feeling, and impulse.

The Broadened Span of Child Population

Apart from the fact that children are themselves changing, teachers are being called upon to work with a changed group of children, that is, with a stratum of the child population whose presence in school was barely visible and hardly acknowledged a generation ago. Children of the previous generation who seemed less ready or able to perform and behave in school according to established academic expectations and standards, that is, those from culturally and economically disadvantaged homes and minority backgrounds, were simply passed over and shunted aside. However, as a result of a new national commitment, buttressed by legislation, to provide equality of educational opportunity and of greater self-assertiveness and heightened consciousness among members of ethnic minorities as well as changing demographic trends, there are greater numbers of children in school from family backgrounds and households whose style of living and cultural values diverge from previously established behavior standards and expectations.

The gap between behavioral expectations at home and in school makes it more difficult for children outside of the mainstream of society to adapt to school. The classroom arouses in them a greater sense of alienation and displeasure. With the new egalitarianism, the greater opportunity afforded for self-expression, and the increased numbers of those from more alien backgrounds, there are many more children disposed to dislike school and even larger numbers who are now freer to voice their rebellious and impatient feelings. As these oppositional attitudes toward school gain more open expression, the atmosphere of the classroom becomes suffused in overtones of mutiny and resistiveness that further undermine the maintenance of academic standards. It breeds a demoralization among students and teachers that makes it more difficult to pursue serious academic goals.

Another factor that is likely to complicate the education of young children is the increasing variability of their intellectual backgrounds. Because preschool programs are small and tend to serve particular communities, the children enrolled in a given program are likely to be relatively homogeneous with regard to family background and ability level. If preschool education becomes universal and more centrally located, teachers will encounter child groups with more heterogeneous backgrounds. Moreover, the dramatic increase in knowledge about the world now available to children, as well as the increased rates of stimulation to which they are exposed, are likely to extend still further the heterogeneity of ability and knowledge of school children. Children vary in their access to and ability to process and integrate the rich flow of information to which they are exposed—television, travel, and the vast array of educational toys and reading material now available to them. Thus, teachers have to be prepared to deal with a greater range of variation of knowledge and abilities among children and a wider range of response patterns to the demands of school.

SOME ISSUES

In contemplating the projected expansion of preschool and the progressively earlier and more widespread exposure of children to institutional, substitutive forms of child care, a number of issues and questions emerge: What are the potential gains and losses to the young child of earlier universal education? How is the opportunity to attend preschool likely to affect the subsequent school careers of children? What will be the effects of increasing availability of substitutive forms of child care on the commitment to parenting?

Effects of Earlier Separation

At first glance, the rapid growth and downward (in age) extension of preschool would appear to represent a resounding victory for the field of early education, a public endorsement of the value of their "product," so to speak. As has been claimed and demonstrated over the years, early education can help to prepare children to respond more effectively to the challenges of later schooling. Especially to the child who comes from a minority family background and who may therefore appear from the perspective of public education to be culturally different, the opportunity to attend preschool will provide additional language experience and help to bring about greater familiarity with the social framework of classroom life and with the tools of learning that are used in school. Early education, when properly delivered, helps to generate a sense of comfort and safety in a school setting that allows children to feel more relaxed in school; it frees them to explore and fantasize and to become invested in learning.

On the other hand, we need to be reminded that the body of knowledge and psychodynamic developmental theory that has helped to articulate the value of early education and how it can most effectively be implemented is the same theoretical framework that has contributed to our understanding of the nature of the vulnerability of young children and to the long-term consequences of responses to stress during the early years. Building on their own observations of young children and the theoretical analysis of Bowlby (1969, 1973) and other psychodynamic writers, educators of young children are acutely aware of the nature of separation problems and of their enduring impact. In contemplating earlier and universal education for young children, we need to ask whether such early experiences of institutionalized care will be in the best interests of most children (see Fraiberg, 1977, for a less sanguine appraisal of current trends to send younger and younger children to day care).

Issues of the vulnerability of young children and the need to provide them with a protective environment are not raised in connection with such extreme, recently publicized, but improbable dangers as physical and sexual abuse, real as they may be in some rare instances. They refer, instead, to the idea that most new and strange environments, because of the new demands they make on the child's adaptive capacities, the disruptions and discontinuities they introduce, and the challenges they pose, are likely to cause distress in young children. By virtue of their immaturity young children have a more limited ability to understand the basis for the stress that they may experience and are less able to deal with it effectively. Depending on the child's repertoire of coping mechanisms, stress may call forth forms of adaptation that involve costly and restrictive modes of defense that may have enduring deleterious consequences.

The stress experienced by the child may have more to do with discrepancies between what is experienced at home and the way in which life in the preschool setting is organized than with the noxious quality of actual treatment in preschool. At the same time, given the comparatively small number of well-trained preschool teachers now available and the rate at which the demand for preschool teachers will increase, unless there is a corresponding willingness to pay for the expertise and educational framework (i.e., teacher : pupil ratio, physical plant, etc.) that is required to deliver first-rate early education, there are solid grounds for concern that the forthcoming expansion of early education will not be sufficiently responsive to the needs and vulnerabilities of young children.

When preschool is not properly implemented or is delivered to children not yet ready for it, when they are asked too early to deal with a strange adult and the child group, it can leave them with feelings of helplessness, of having been left too soon to their own devices, of having been abandoned. If children cannot cope with such a situation, they may respond by walling off the menacing stimuli of an alien environment. Their efforts to protect themselves may isolate them from the main stimulation of school and thereby minimize their responsiveness to school. This restrictive mode of defending against the onslaughts of school may be sustained throughout the school career and, moreover, may be generalized to other challenging environments as well.

Universal Preschool in the Public Schools

There is a danger that universal preschool education, when conducted under the auspices of the public schools, will alter the character of early education — partly by virtue of the bureaucratic quality of the public schools that is likely to change the emotional climate of the preschool classroom and the traditional academic focus of public schools. If and when preschools are appended to elementary school and ultimately absorbed by them, as now seems probable, they will become incorporated into a body of educational thinking and programming that is primarily concerned with academic instruction. Moreover, since public education has traditionally dealt with older children, early education will be under the aegis of educators who are for the most part unknowing about the developmental needs of young children, about what young children need to know and how they learn.

The impact of earlier universal schooling will in large measure depend on the purposes that it is viewed by the public schools as serving. Does the institution of universal preschool signal the adoption by the schools of a developmental view of children, and will preschool be given over to enriching the children's development during these earlier formative stages that will enhance their capacity to respond to growth-supporting and stimulating experiences in later years? Or will preschool be used to begin the educational life cycle sooner with the idea that some of the mounting restlessness of older children can be forestalled by gaining their release from school to the labor force earlier?

Nor is it plausible to believe that most educational deficiencies stem from insufficient exposure to academic instruction. It is doubtful that there will be a beneficial outcome when children are immersed in an academic regimen that is not achieving its desired results at a point in time when they are even less ready to cope with it than when they are older. The situation will be worsened if the public schools come to regard preschool as a way of simply initiating children to the academic regimen earlier, as a means of forestalling the widespread apathy and low scholastic performance now encountered by gaining additional time to deliver academic instruction. Under such circumstances, the stresses associated with preschool are likely to be magnified. For these reasons, the current readiness to expand preschool education must be tempered by thoughtful awareness of the vulnerability of young children and what is best for them.

Changing Patterns of Responsiveness to School

When properly implemented, early education can promote the development of curiosity and provide experience with the tools for learning that will foster a sense of industry and inquisitiveness that supports academic learning. On the other hand, when preschool programs are largely custodial and children begin to attend them at an early age, and when the multiple functions performed by the school include providing meals and periods of leisure and rest, it may be difficult for children to associate school with serious work and for teachers to engage children in rigorous exploration and learning. In effect, many children may come to think of school as a place where one mainly passes time and "hangs out" with friends.

Teachers believe that the school-age child has a shorter attention span and is less motivated to learn than were the children of an earlier generation. Today's children are also seen as more questioning and challenging of authority and as less willing to exert effort unless presented with reasons that are associated with tangible rewards. In light of these trends, if children are to begin attending school at an earlier age, it will be especially important for them to be helped to understand that school is a place where they work, even if children's work is play. At school the business is learning, learning is important, and children are learners. These are themes that need to be conveyed to young children in age-appropriate ways to make school seem challenging and exciting, without plunging them into regimented classrooms with lessons that are not suitable for young children.

Although children tend to begin school at an earlier age, teachers appear to be less salient figures in their life. Early schooling brings children together sooner and allows them to spend time out from under their mother's thumb and away from the family. Gains in self-reliance and early entry into the peer group have always been valued as among the major achievements of early education. However, young children of today present images of sophistication, worldliness, and independence that make it more difficult for the teacher to reach them. Similarly, the peer group becomes a salient force in the lives of children at an earlier age. The net effect is the emergence of a pattern of lessened responsiveness to adults, a diminished readiness to identify with adults and to learn from them. Thus, investment in the peer group has come to mean a flight from the influence of adults and, more than in the past, to serve as a vehicle for becoming disconnected from the adult world. For these reasons, it would seem important for early education to reassess and modulate its traditional concern with drawing children into the peer group.

Commitment to Parenting

Universal early education is a powerful emancipating force for women. Given the social and technological changes that have altered the need for mothers to stay home, early education offers a vehicle that frees mothers, or at least provides much greater flexibility, in the arena of perhaps their greatest responsibility, that of child care. In so doing, however, it may also contribute to the erosion of commitment to parenting and an abnegation of parental responsibility. Early education frees women to cope with pressing economic problems and supports their career aspirations and their search for self-fulfillment, but it may also contribute to the abandonment of children, and to a reduction of the actual readiness and perceived need to provide support and guidance for children. Insofar as early education makes it easier for adults to retreat from their parenting responsibilities, it may sow the seeds for a rootlessness that interferes with the very learning process and development of competence that it was designed to promote.

OVERVIEW

In examining the current status of children and exploring the implications of the actual and projected expansion of preschool, we must recognize that it is less possible to be protective of children than in the recent past. It is more difficult to shield them from events and phenomena that we believe to be disturbing or confusing to the young child. As a result, we have come to reassess the urgency and the feasibility of maintaining such protectiveness and have, instead, assigned importance to the need to strengthen children psychologically, to enable them to withstand the stresses of modern life.

Similarly, it is becoming increasingly difficult to arrange for young children to grow up under the exclusive care of their parents in the familiar and safe environment of their homes. Even if there were agreement among child development experts, — which there is not — that it is best for young children to be home and to be taken care of by their parents, there are large numbers of children who must attend some form of preschool because their parents are unable or unwilling to care for them. Clearly, more and better preschool facilities are needed to accommodate the needs of such families. What remains unclear is whether these increasing patterns of special needs mean that educational programs and policies with regard to all children should be changed in order to meet the changing patterns of special needs of particular families.

As we lower the age at which children first attend school and make preschool increasingly available, we need to bear in mind the special vulnerability of young children to the stresses of early exposure to an alien, less protective environment. Further, as parents increasingly become unavailable to care for their children we need to understand what this reduced availability means for the child and to monitor the impact of substitute child care resources on the commitment to parenting.

Children are growing up more independently from birth, and they are growing more rapidly, but the pattern of acceleration is uneven. Their relation to school and adults and to one another is in flux. Some of our previous images of the developing fabric of the child are themselves outmoded. It is time to reassess issues of the impact of early education in the context of a revised vision of the status of children and their development during this period of rapid social and technological change. At the same time, we cannot wish away what is known about the developmental needs and vulnerabilities of young children.

REFERENCES

Biber, B. (1934). A nursery school puts psychology to work. *69 Bank Street, 1* (3), 1–11.

Biber, B. (1984). *Early education and psychological development*. New Haven: Yale University Press.

Bowlby, J. (1969). *Attachment and loss, I: Attachment*. New York: Basic Books.

Bowlby, J. (1973). *Attachment and loss, II: Separation*. New York: Basic Books.

Fraiberg, S. (1977). *Every child's birthrights: In defense of mothering*. New York: Basic Books.

Isaacs, S. (1936). *The nursery years*. New York: Vanguard Press.

Zigler, E., & Valentine, J. (Eds.). (1979). *Project Headstart*. New York: Free Press.

Zimiles, H. (1984). *The changing American child: Final report*. New York: William T. Grant Foundation.

Zimiles, H. (1985, April). The role of research in an era of expanding preschool education. Paper presented at the American Educational Research Association, Chicago.

CHAPTER 2

Bilingual Development and the Education of Bilingual Children During Early Childhood

Eugene E. García

The issues surrounding bilingualism are of specific interest to a large bilingual segment (Mexican American, Chinese, Haitian, Native American, Puerto Rican, Cajun, Vietnamese, etc.) of this nation's population (U.S. Commission on Civil Rights, 1974) and of general interest to students of language acquisition (McNeil, 1966). Other reviews of bilingualism and second-language acquisition have dealt with the definition of bilingualism, linguistic overlap, linguistic "interference," cognitive interaction, and theoretical issues related to each of these areas (see MacNamara, 1967; Cummins, 1979; Garcia, 1983). The purpose of the present review is to discuss some of these issues in light of more recent research and applied information specific to bilingual development in young children, with special attention to bilingualism in the United States. Therefore, this review will (1) provide some functional information related to the social, linguistic, and psychological character of bilingual children and (2) provide certain recommendations related to the education of bilingual students, particularly at the kindergarten level.

The term *early childhood bilingualism* suggests the acquisition of two languages during the first 5 years of life. This definition includes the following conditions:

1. Children are *able to comprehend and produce* linguistic aspects of two languages.
2. Children are *exposed "naturally," in the form of social interaction, to the two languages* as they are used during early childhood. This condition requires a substantive bilingual environment. In many cases this exposure comes from within a nuclear-and-extended-family network, but this need not be the case (visitors and

extended visits to foreign countries are examples of alternative environments).

3. *Development must be simultaneous* in both languages. This is contrasted with the case of a native speaker of one language, who after mastery of that language, begins on a course of second-language acquisition.

The above definition stresses the importance of the acquisition of two languages within social contexts during a very significant cognitive development period. The remainder of this chapter attempts to address issues related to the social context in which the development occurs, the character of that development, the cognitive consequences of the development, and the possible educational implications related to schooling. For purposes of discussion, social, linguistic, and cognitive attributes of bilingualism will be separated; however, these processes are interactive in nature. Such an interactive framework characterizes best the complexity of bilingual development and the education of bilingual children during early childhood.

SOCIAL CONTEXT

As Riegel (1968) suggests, any chronological record of children's linguistic output coupled with linguistic input information would allow an important correlational analysis of language development. Although such extensive information remains unavailable, some systematic semblance of this type of data is becoming available for monolingual English-speaking children (Brown & Fraser, 1963; Schacter, Kirshner, Klips, Freidericks, & Sanders, 1974). Unfortunately, little information of this caliber is available for young bilingual children.

Although this absence of empirical data is crippling, some cautious notions of bilingual input seem justifiable. If one considers the eventual bilingual character of the child, it seems appropriate to suggest that some percentage of the child's linguistic information is in one language and some other percentage is in a second language. One might tie the acquisition of either language to the general theoretical notion of "degree of linguistic input." Mathematically, the extent of bilingualism would be directly related to the proportion of language information made available.

This simple relationship must be qualified because of several theoretical and empirical considerations. Edelman (1969) reports the differential use of Spanish and English vocabulary in Puerto Rican children on a word-naming task as a function of the different contexts (school, home, neighborhood, church) the children were asked to describe. Skrabanek (1970) in a study of Spanish maintenance among Mexican Americans, found that the use of Spanish differed as a function of the age of the speaker. Older subjects spoke more often in Spanish, although both young and old alike used Spanish a substantial proportion of the time. Kuo (1974) reports that the differential use of language by Chinese American children was related to age and other socialization variables.

Language is learned within a child's culture, and children coming from different cultures will use language in ways that reflect their different cultures. This is particularly the case for bilingual children, children in whom social functioning takes place in two languages. For example, a child from a Mexican American or Native American family will not necessarily talk about the same things, or use language to accomplish the same functions, as a child from an urban black or Anglo family. The key term here is *language use*. It is important to distinguish between the *form* of a child's language and the *function* served by that language. Language form (phonology, syntax, grammar, and vocabulary) has been the traditional focus of language intervention for children. More than a decade ago, William Labov (1970) identified this duality in his own research and delineated two aspects of the problem:

1. Structural conflicts of standard and nonstandard English: interference with learning ability stemming from a mismatch of linguistic structures.
2. Functional conflicts of standard and nonstandard English: interference with the desire to learn standard English stemming from a mismatch in the functions that standard and nonstandard English perform in a given culture (p. 6).

Labov's research focused on both of these issues, and he identified numerous functional conflicts between the nonstandard English of the urban black children he studied and the standard English demanded by the school. Duran (1981) and García (1983) as well as others provide a wealth of similar information for Spanish-English bilingual populations. Unfortunately, curriculum developers and language testers are often slow to take advantage of these results. For example, Labov found that many of the children he studied were unwilling to answer questions to which the questioner obviously knew the answer. An adult, holding up a picture of a helicopter and saying to a child, "What's this?" is likely to get either no answer or, "I don't know." It is impossible to say in this situation whether the child really doesn't know or whether the child is reasoning, "That question is too easy. Anybody knows what that is. There must be some catch to this. I will protect myself by not answering until I know more about what's going on here." This protection strategy is frequently employed by urban black children, and yet their silences or "don't know" answers are interpreted as evidence of cognitive or language delay. Genishi (1981), in a study of bilingual Mexican American children in California, gives further weight to Labov's example. She points out that the children in her study switch languages (from English to Spanish or vice versa) depending on their own impressions of the listener's "strongest" language. She reports that what seemed at first glance a disturbed language-switching situation became a systematic interactional discourse strategy that maximized communication.

Therefore, this willingness to use more than one language in performance situations can cause real problems in traditional testing situations where it is clear that there is one right language and the tester knows what it is.

Functional Language

A functional approach to language acquisition is not a recent development. Cazden (1970) refers to a functional view of language — a focus on how the child brings language to bear on meeting the demands of the situations in which language is used. The key to this approach is the notion that grammatical structure cannot be understood outside the context in which language is used (Bloom, 1970). The functionalist approach to language holds that grammar is a secondary or derived system, related to the constraints of the communication task. As Bates (1976, p. 23) indicates, "the child's acquisition of grammar is guided, not by abstract categories, but by the pragmatic and semantic structure of communications interacting with the performance constraint of the speech channel." The child's task is one of mapping a diverse set of semantic and pragmatic functions onto a set of grammatical forms. A functional approach suggests children concentrate first on *what they can do with language.*

With such a view, cultural diversity in language use becomes increasingly significant. In other words, a functional approach makes us interested in what Hymes (1967) calls the child's "communicative competence" — that is, the child's knowledge of rules of speaking meaningfully. If we wish to assist in developing a child's knowledge of constructs beyond subject-verb agreement and past-tense verbs, if we want to know whether children can use language functionally in the environment, then we need a nontraditional language view. Moreover, even if we wish to identify and implement instructional procedures related to "linguistic competence," our methods must be inherently linked to communicative functions.

Useful accounts of early childhood bilingualism must, therefore, take into consideration more than the child's linguistic ability. They must consider the child's surrounding environment. The environmental context will determine:

1. The specific linguistic and metalinguistic information important for the development of each language
2. The specific social language-use rules for each language
3. The specific linguistic and sociolinguistic rules governing code switching
4. The prestige of the language and, therefore, the "motivation" to learn and maintain or ignore and dissipate language differentially.

This form of analysis is one of the most needed within the bilingual research domain. It is also one that holds much promise in providing information drawn directly from bilingual acquisition but also of importance to the understanding of language acquisition in general. For as McNeil (1966) has indicated, differential development of specific language features in the course of bilingual acquisition may very well signal important relationships between that differential development and sociocultural variables.

BILINGUAL DEVELOPMENT

The previous discussion related to language function does not negate the significance of language "form" development. Much research has centered on the form of single-language development (Brown & Fraser, 1963), and other research has employed comparative linguistic analysis with children who are learning different languages (Bowerman, 1975; Braine, 1976). A much smaller set of systematic investigations is available regarding children who are developing more than one language, simultaneously, during the early part of their lives.

Sorenson (1967) describes the acquisition of three to four languages by young children who live in the Northwest Amazon region of South America. In this Brazilian-Colombian border region, the Tukano tribal language serves as the *lingua franca*, but some 25 other clearly distinguishable linguistic groups continue to exist. In the United States, Skrabanek (1970) reports the continued acquisition and support of both English and Spanish language systems among preschool children of the Southwest; this phenomenon has existed for the past hundred years with no indication that it will be disrupted.

Ronjat (1913) reports the development of French and German in his own son, when one parent consistently spoke French and the other German. Finding little deleterious effect of bilingual development, he attributed the positive outcome to the separation of the languages. Pavlovitch (1920) also reports the development of two languages, French and Serbian, in his son. Similarly, languages were separated across individuals and the language developed simultaneously with minimal confusion. Geissler (1938) reports, anecdotally, that as a teacher of foreign languages he has observed young children acquire up to four languages simultaneously without apparent difficulty. However, Smith (1935), in a study of missionary families who spoke English and Chinese, reports difficulty during simultaneous acquisition. This difficulty was most apparent in the language mixing that characterized some children's speech.

One of the first systematic investigations of bilingual acquisition in young children was reported by Leopold (1947, 1949). This author set out to study the simultaneous acquisition of English and German in his own child. These initial descriptive reports indicate that as the subject was exposed to both languages during infancy, she seemed to weld both languages into one system during the initial language-production periods. For instance, early language forms were characterized by free mixing. Language production during later periods seemed to indicate that the use of English and German grammatical forms developed independently.

More recent studies have systematically addressed several issues relevant to bilingual acquisition. Carrow (1971, 1972) restricted her study to the receptive domain of young bilingual Mexican American children in the Southwest. A comparison of English and Spanish comprehension on comprehension tasks for bilinguals (Carrow, 1971) revealed that (1) linguistically, children were heterogeneous; some scored better in one language than another and others were equal in both; (2) a greater proportion of children scored higher in English than in Spanish; and (3) older children scored higher on these measures in both languages. (This was the case even though Spanish was not used as a medium of instruction for children who were in educational programs).

García (1983) reports developmental data related to the acquisition of Spanish and English for Spanish-English bilingual preschoolers (3–4 years old) and the acquisition of English for a group of matched English-only speakers. The results of that study can be summarized as follows: (1) acquisition of both Spanish and English was evident at complex morphological (grammatical) and syntactic levels for Spanish-English 4-year-old children; (2) for the bilingual children studied, English was more advanced based on the quantity and quality of obtained morphological and syntactic instances of language production; and (3) there was no quantitative or qualitative difference between Spanish-English bilingual children and matched English-only controls on English-language production.

Huerta (1977) has provided a report of a longitudinal analysis for a Spanish-English bilingual 2-year-old child. She reports a similar pattern of continuous Spanish-English development, although identifiable stages appeared in which one language forged ahead of the other. Moreover, she reports the significant occurrence of mixed-language utterances that made use of both Spanish and English lexicon as well as Spanish and English morphology. In all cases these mixed linguistic utterances were well formed and communicative. García, Maez, and González (1981), in a national study of bilingual children 4, 5, and 6 years of age, found regional differences in the relative occurrence of switched language utterances. That is, bilingual Spanish-English children from Texas, Arizona, Colorado, and New Mexico showed higher (15%–20%) incidences of language-switched utterances than children from California, Illinois, New York, or Florida, especially at prekindergarten levels. These findings suggest that some children may develop an "interlanguage" in addition to the acquisition of two independent language systems later in development.

The above "developmental" findings can be capsulized succinctly but not without acknowledging their tentative nature:

1. The acquisition of more than one language during early childhood is a documented phenomenon.
2. The acquisition of two languages can be parallel but need not be. That is, the qualitative character of one language may lag behind, surge ahead, or develop equally with the other language.
3. The acquisition of two languages may very well result in an interlanguage incorporating the aspects (lexicon, morphology, and syntax) of both languages.
4. The acquisition of two languages need not hamper, developmentally, the acquisition of either language.

Of course, these conclusions are very broad in character. The specific nature of bilingual development and its causal links to environmental variables remain unavailable.

INTELLIGENCE, COGNITION, AND BILINGUALISM

Cognitive processes are also related to bilingual acquisition in early childhood. Based on information relating early childhood bilingualism to decreased performance on standardized tests of intelligence, a causal statement linking bilingualism to depressed intelligence is tempting. Although this pervasive negative relationship appears in much early work (Darcy, 1953), the methodological problem of studies investigating this type of relationship are serious, and any conclusions concerning bilingualism and intellectual functioning (as measured by standardized individual or group intelligence tests) must be extremely tentative (Darcy, 1963).

With the general shift away from standardized measures of intelligence, the information processing of bilingual children as it is related to specific areas of cognitive development has received attention. Leopold (1949), in one of the first investigations of bilingual acquisition with young children, reported a general cognitive plasticity for his young bilingual subject. He suggested that linguistic flexibility (in the form of bilingualism) generalized to nonlinguistic, cognitive tasks. Peal and Lambert (1962), in a summarization of their work with French-English bilinguals and English monolinguals, suggested that the intellectual experience of acquiring two languages contributed to an advantageous mental flexibility, superior concept formation, and a generally diversified set of mental abilities. Padilla (1977) reasoned that bilinguals must be cognitively advanced because they are able to process information provided in one language and produce allied information in another language. (I refer here to the ability of a child to understand a problem statement in one language, solve that problem, and produce the answer in a second language). For example, Keats and Keats (1974) report a study in which German-English bilinguals who did not exemplify weight conservation were trained to conserve in one of the two languages. Results from English and German posttests indicated that the concept was acquired in both languages. This suggests the possible increased flexibility of bilinguals during conceptual acquisition.

Feldman and Shen (1971), Ianco-Worrall (1972), Carringer (1974), and Cummins and Gulatson (1974) have begun to provide relevant evidence in this regard. Feldman and Shen (1971) report differential responding between Spanish-English bilinguals and English monolinguals across three separate cognitive tasks. The first, an object-constancy task, required subjects to identify an object (a cup) after its shape had been altered (smashed) in their presence. The second, a nonsense-labeling and switched-name task, required subjects to label familiar items either with nonsense words (e.g., *wug*) or to switch the names of these familiar items (e.g., label a cup a glass and vice versa). The third, an associative sentence task, required subjects to use familiar, nonsense, and switched labels (of the second task) in a sentence describing a relation between the labeled items ("the wug is on the plate"). Results indicated significantly increased cognitive flexibility for bilinguals. Ianco-Worrall (1972) compared matched bilinguals (Afrikaans-English) and monolingual (either Afrikaans or English) on separation of word-sound, word-meaning tasks. Comparison of scores on these tasks indicated that bilinguals concentrated more on attaching meaning to words than to sounds.

In an attempt to identify more specifically the relationship between cognition and bilingualism, Cummins (1979; 1981) has proposed an interactive theoretical proposition: that children who achieve "balanced proficiency" in two languages are advantaged cognitively in comparison with monolingual children, and that children who do not achieve balanced proficiency in two languages (but who are immersed in a bilingual environment) are cognitively disadvantaged in comparison to monolingual and balanced proficient bilinguals. This formulation presents most directly the shift away from a disadvantaged perspective (Darcy, 1953, 1963) to an advantaged perspective while at the same time continuing to consider the potential negative influence of (unbalanced) bilingualism. This interactionist position attempts to account for the success of Canadian French immersion bilingual programs for English-speaking children and the failure of English immersion programs for Spanish-speaking children in the United States.

García (1983) takes issue with this interactionist conceptualization on several grounds. First, the data to support the interactionist position are primarily Canadian. Second, these same data have previously been criticized on a more severe subject-selection criterion. It is likely that only high-achieving and highly intelligent children were selected for inclusion into bilingual education groupings. Therefore, cognitive advantages that may have already existed prior to bilingual "instruction" may have contributed to the success of bilingual development, not vice versa. Moreover, successful subjects came from either majority, middle, or high socioeconomic strata where education was valued and learning a second language was openly rewarded. Learning a second language under such conditions is quite different from one dictated by economic depression as well as social and psychological repression of a minority language culture. In sum, it is not necessary to account for differences in bilinguals' (balanced or not) and monolinguals' cognitive performance on the basis of a cognitively advantaged-disadvantaged conceptualization. Instead, it remains possible that individual differences in intellectual functioning, combined with the support or nonsupport of the social context for acquiring linguistic and academic skills, are the factors responsible for any specific differences in bilingual and monolingual performance on cognitive measures.

In sum, any detailed conclusion concerning the relationship between the bilingual character of children and cognitive functioning must remain tentative. It is the case that:

1. Bilingual children have been found to score both higher and lower than monolingual children on specific and general measures of cognitive development, intelligence, and school achievement.
2. "Balanced" bilinguals have outperformed monolinguals and "unbalanced" bilinguals on specific cognitive tasks.
3. Specific hypotheses relating bilingualism to cognitive and intellectual functioning have been advanced (Darcy, 1953, 1963; Cummins, 1979).

Like so much of the data in the bilingual area, these data must be perceived as tentative and must be considered further evidence of the need for more specific research concerning the relationship between language and cognition.

EDUCATIONAL IMPLICATIONS FOR BILINGUAL EDUCATION IN EARLY CHILDHOOD

It is almost universally accepted that language and social repertoire have their origins in early childhood years. It seems that almost all of the basic linguistic skills (phonology, morphology, syntax) of adult language as well as important personal and social attributes (self-concept, social identity, social interaction styles) are significantly influenced during these years. Consequently, one motive for early educational intervention has been the potential removal of barriers related to the development of these important linguistic, psychological, and social attributes. With respect to early childhood programs for bilinguals, it would be important to recognize the linguistic and cultural character of these children in any such effort. In 1974, the U.S. Commission on Civil Rights spoke directly to issues of language diversity and education by stressing the importance of early childhood instruction incorporating the native language of the children it serves. Put directly, the instructional staff must be able to communicate in the child's native language, and the instructional curriculum must also significantly reflect the child's native language.

> When language is recognized as the means for representing thought, and as the vehicle for complex thinking, the importance of allowing children to use and develop the language they know best becomes obvious. (U.S. Commission on Civil Rights, 1974, p. 44)

In line with the above recommendation, the Administration for Children, Youth, and Families of the Department of Health and Human Services initiated a national effort to assist local Head Start centers to "implement and develop bilingual-bicultural programs" (Arenas, 1978). Efforts were aimed at four areas: curriculum development, staff training, resource network development, and research and evaluation of curriculum development and implementation efforts. The results of the evaluation of these curriculum development efforts are now available (Sandoval-Martínez, 1982). As this evaluation has reported, instruction of bilingual Spanish-dominant preschool children in their native language and English was significantly superior to the education of a matched group of children who received instruction only in English. As Williams (1978) concluded, bilingual education is a natural extension of the maturing of early childhood education and will hold a prominent position in future years.

The bilingual education legislation of 1967–1968 began a nationwide trend of great significance. Like many educational trends, this one had as its impetus social and political forces. It was not based on a long history of sound empirical research related to bilingual development and bilingual education. Instead, it was a movement reflecting a new hope for bilingual populations who had previously been ignored. It was never clear that bilingual education would provide effective educational programming, but it was clear that the "traditional" programs were unsuccessful. Some 10 to 15 years after this initiative, it seems appropriate to at least briefly review this endeavor and its relationship to specific and related empirical research that it has directly or indirectly spawned. In doing so, it is important to be reminded of the investigatory paradox: empirical investigations (research) of applied educational phenomena most often generate more "new" questions without having provided substantive answers to questions they were meant to address. Research in bilingual education is no exception to this paradox.

Teaching and Learning Strategies

It is always difficult to extract from a body of research literature specific implications for an applied teaching technology. The character of controlled research environments, the uncharacteristic control of intervening variables, and the formality of independent variable intervention often preclude generalization of findings to "real" classrooms. Yet from these study environments of controlled experimentation and observation information potentially of relevance to bilingual classrooms has emerged. McLaughlin's (1978) review of such led him to conclude that many misconceptions are prevalent with respect to second-language and bilingual acquisition in early childhood. Among them:

1. The young child acquires a language more quickly and easily than an adult because the child is biologically programmed to acquire language, whereas the adult is not.
2. The younger the child, the more skilled he is in acquiring a second language.
3. Second language acquisition is a qualitatively different process than first language acquisition.
4. Interferences between first and second language is an inevitable and ubiquitous part of second language acquisition.
5. There is a single method of second-language instruction that is most effective with all children.
6. The experience of bilingualism negatively (or positively) affects the child's intellectual development, language skills, educational attainment, emotional adjustment and/or cognitive functioning. (McLaughlin, 1978, pp. 197–205)

McLaughlin is not admitting total ignorance in concluding that the above propositions are false. Instead, he is following the strategy of any good scientist: Propositions that are extracted from empirical observation and experimentation are to be handled with extreme caution and doubt. It is possible that some or all of the above propositions are true, but to claim their truth at a time when supportive evidence is unavailable is unwarranted and clearly not in the best interest of future research and the applied technology of education.

Is it possible to answer any bilingual education concerns? With the issue of caution in mind, there are some questions specifically related to bilingual education and bilingual research that deserve discussion.

Will bilingual education efforts in early childhood negatively affect children's linguistic and cognitive development? Given the data discussed previously, it seems clear that exposure to two languages does not retard linguistic or cognitive development. That is, children who were operating at complex levels in Spanish were not "retarded" in English as compared to other matched monolingual English-speaking children. Moreover, bilingual preschool children did not score lower on measures of cognitive development than their matched monolingual English peers. Therefore, a bilingual experience in early childhood alone does not necessarily retard linguistic or cognitive development. Unfortunately, important questions still remain, such as (1) How are differences in the qualitative nature of the bilingual experience related to linguistic and cognitive development? and (2) How are cognitive-process variables related to bilingual development?

Do bilingual education efforts in early childhood positively affect linguistic and cognitive development? Although there is evidence for the lack of negative effects of bilingual acquisition on general linguistic development, there is no evidence of advanced linguistic development for bilinguals when compared to matched monolinguals. That is, there is no report of bilingual students' increased proficiency in either language as compared to native monolingual speakers of either language. Cognitively, there is evidence that bilinguals score significantly higher on several cognitive measures than matched monolingual peers. These measures tend to be those reflecting the ability to consider properties of the environment in a more "flexible" manner: to construct more general semantic categories than monolingual peers. The following critical questions remain:

1. Are these advantages related to bilingualism or other (potentially cultural) variables associated with bilingualism?
2. Are these advantages related to proficiency levels of bilingualism?
3. Are these advantages related to the specific languages involved and specific cognitive measures (tasks)?

To what extent should education efforts for bilingual children utilize their native language and English? It seems evident from the foregoing review that many critical issues related to bilingual development and the education of bilingual students remain unresolved. Contradictory research findings have emerged regarding the qualitative nature of bilingual development, although this form of research is not new. Moreover, cognitive correlates of bilingualism have only recently begun to receive systematic attention at the empirical level. Formal evaluation of bilingual instruction models has proven to be a difficult and often disappointing enterprise (Troike, 1981). Only the Canadian bilingual French-English programs have provided thorough and comprehensive evaluation information. Unfortunately, due to critical ethnolinguistic, socioeconomic, and sociopolitical differences regarding the context of the Canadian programs, the results of those evaluations are impossible to relate to ongoing bilingual education programs for minority ethnolinguistic groups of the United States.

Besides reemphasizing the need for more and better basic and applied research in the area of bilingualism and bilingual instruction, what recommendations regarding instructional procedures for the education for bilingual students might be made? First, the previous discussion of research has emphasized the interaction of linguistic, cognitive, and social domains. That is, *bilingual* children must be perceived as developing linguistic, social, and cognitive attributes interdependently. Therefore, a bilingual child brings to the schooling environment two linguistic systems and a history of immersion within a complex social milieu utilizing those two systems at a time when cognitive and academic growth is most

influenced by the social milieu. It seems reasonable to suggest that it is
these different social milieus which have produced the discrepancies in
research outcomes discussed previously. And, since the classroom is a
systematic extension of these social-interaction patterns, it will either serve
to enhance or impede continued linguistic, social, and cognitive development.

How might the classroom serve to enhance that development? Linguistic ability is the first key variable, although alone it is not of independent importance. Recall that bilinguals possess diverse linguistic functioning repertoires: (1) the child may be more proficient in L_1 than L_2 (the
dominant L_1 child); (2) the child may be equally proficient in L_1 and L_2
(the balanced bilingual child). Proficiency here is meant to take into consideration the broader definition of communicative competence rather
than standard "morphological and syntactic" competence. If effective instruction is to take place in classrooms, communication between student
and teacher must be maximized. Most directly, this mandates instruction in the child's dominant language. Where English is not the student's
dominant language, academic instruction should not reflect an English
emphasis. Specific evidence from the Head Start bilingual evaluation supports this recommendation (Sandoval-Martínez, 1982).

Should English be taught at all in these educational environments?
In almost all regions of the country, English pervades the child's natural
social and educational environment. The physical presence and the psychological weight of such a presence impels English development. Therefore, although some English-as-a-second-language (ESL) instruction may
be beneficial, it is unlikely that a child exposed to such a limited English
environment will become proficient in this language. Of course, this acquisition will take time. By moving forward with academic instruction
in the child's dominant language, however, no academic or cognitive
retardation is likely to result.

The balanced bilingual presents a different educational challenge.
This student is exceptional and should be considered gifted. Therefore,
instruction for this child should reflect this exceptionality. Instruction
should emphasize both languages wherever possible. Ten years ago bilingual instruction of balanced bilinguals would have been almost impossible, but with the development of bilingual materials and the training of
bilingual personnel in the last decade, it is not only possible but educationally desirable to maintain and further extend the child's bilingual
competency.

For the unbalanced, English-dominant student, instruction should
reflect this English proficiency. This is not to suggest that bilingual instruction for these students should be unavailable. These children bring

their ethnolinguistic status to the English curriculum. It is important, psychologically, not to negate this ethnolinguistic consciousness. Bilingual instruction should emphasize the inseparable nature of culture and language, with some systematic L_2-as-a-second-language instruction. The goal of this form of instruction model would be not to produce proficient bilinguals but instead to explore culturally and linguistically the ethnolinguistic heritage of the student in order to maximize the educational influence of the classroom.

The above commentary regarding classroom policy is based on the scarcity of sound empirical research currently available, and it is consistent with the present knowledge base regarding multilingual acquisition. The commentary is made with regard to early schooling years, particularly kindergarten, a period of critical importance for establishing effective instructional programming. This is especially true for children from ethnolinguistic minority groups whose educational history has been riddled with neglect and failure. For these children bilingual instruction in its various forms holds the promise of educational parity.

REFERENCES

Arenas, S. (1978, July–August). Bilingual/bicultural programs for preschool children. *Children Today*, 43–48.

Bates, E. (1976). *Language and context*. New York: Academic Press.

Bloom, L. (1970). *Language development: Form and function in emerging grammars*. Boston: MIT Press.

Bowerman, M. (1975). Crosslinguistic similarities at two stages of syntactic development. In E. Lenneberg & E. Lenneberg, (Eds.), *Foundations of language development*. (pp. 173–201). London: UNESCO Press.

Braine, M. D. S. (1976). Children's first word combination. *Monographs of the Society for Research in Child Development*.

Brown, R., & Fraser, D. (1963). The acquisition of syntax. In C. N. Cofer & B. Musgrove (Eds.), *Verbal behavior and learning* (pp. 57–86). New York: McGraw-Hill.

Carringer, D. C. (1974). Creative thinking abilities of Mexican youth: The relationship of bilingualism. *Journal of Cross-Cultural Psychology, 5*, 492–504.

Carrow, E. (1971). Comprehension of English and Spanish by preschool Mexican-American children. *Modern Language Journal, 55*, 299–306.

Carrow, E. (1972). Auditory comprehension of English by monolingual and bilingual preschool children. *Journal of Speech and Hearing Research, 15*, 407–457.

Cazden, C. (1970). The neglected situation in child language research and education. In F. Williams (Ed.), *Language and poverty* (pp. 145–161). Chicago: Markham.

Cummins, J. (1979). Linguistic interdependence and the educational development of bilingual children. *Review of Educational Research, 49*, 222–251.

Cummins, J. (1981). The role of primary language development in promoting
educational success for language minority students. In Calif. State Dept. of
Education (Ed.), *Schooling and language minority students: A theoretical
framework* (pp. 3–50). Los Angeles: Evaluation, Dissemination, and Assessment Center.

Cummins, J., & Gulatson, M. (1974). Bilingual education and cognition. *Alberta
Journal of Education Research, 20*, 259–269.

Darcy, N. T. (1953). A review of the literature of the effects of bilingualism upon
the measurement of intelligence. *Journal of Genetic Psychology, 82*, 21–57.

Darcy, N. T. (1963). Bilingualism and the measurement of intelligence: Review
of a decade of research. *Journal of Genetic Psychology, 103*, 259–282.

Duran, R. (Ed.). (1981). *Latino language and communicative behavior.* Norwood, NJ: Ablex.

Edelman, M. (1969). The contextualization of school children's bilingualism.
Modern Language Journal, 23, 245–258.

Feldman, C., & Shen, M. (1971). Some language related cognitive advantages
of bilingual five-year-olds. *Journal of Genetic Psychology, 118*, 235–244.

García, E. (1983). *Bilingualism in early childhood.* Albuquerque: University of
New Mexico Press.

García, E., Maez, L., & González, G. (1981). A national study of Spanish/English
bilingualism in young Hispanic children of the United States. *Bilingual
Education Paper Series, 4*, 1–37.

Geissler, H. (1938). *Zweisprächigkeit deustcher Kinder im Ausland.* Stuttgart:
Deutscher Kohlhammas.

Genishi, C. (1981). Codeswitching in Chicano six-year-olds. In R. Duran (Ed.),
Latino language and communicative behavior (pp. 133–152). Norwood, NJ:
Ablex.

Huerta, A. (1977, June). The development of codeswitching in a young bilingual.
Working Papers in Sociolinguistics, (21).

Hymes, D. (1967). Models of the interaction of language and social setting. *Journal of Social Issues, 23*, 8–28.

Ianco-Worrall, A. (1972). Bilingualism and cognitive development. *Child Development, 43*, 1390–1400.

Keats, D. M., & Keats, J. A. (1974). The effect of language on concept acquisition in bilingual children. *Journal of Cross-Cultural Psychology, 5*, 80–99.

Kuo, E. C. (1974). The family and bilingual socialization: A sociolinguistic study
of a sample of Chinese children in the United States. *Journal of Social
Psychology, 92*, 181–191.

Labov, W. (1970). *The study of nonstandard English.* Urbana, IL: National
Council of Teachers of English.

Leopold, W. F. (1947). *Speech development of a bilingual child: A linguist's
record: Vol. 1, Vocabulary growth in the first two years.* Evanston, IL:
Northwestern University Press.

Leopold, W. F. (1949). *Speech development of a bilingual child: A linguist's record: Vol. 3, Grammars and general problems in the first two years.* Evanston, IL: Northwestern University Press.

MacNamara, J. (1967). Bilingualism in the modern world. *Journal of Social Issues, 23,* 1–7.

McLaughlin, B. (1978). *Second language acquisition in childhood.* Hillsdale, NJ: Erlbaum.

McNeil, D. (1966). Developmental psycholinguistics. In F. Smith & G. Miller (Eds.), *The genesis of language: A psycholinguistic approach* (pp. 15–84). Cambridge: MIT Press.

Padilla, A. M. (1977). Child bilingualism: Insights to issues. In J. Martínez (Ed.), *Chicano psychology* (pp. 7–29). New York: Academic Press.

Pavlovitch, M. (1920). *Le langage enfantin: Acquisition du serbe et du français par un enfant serbe.* Paris: Champion.

Peal, E., & Lambert, W. E. (1962). The relation of bilingualism to intelligence. *Psychological Monographs: General and Applied, 76*(546), 1–23.

Riegel, K. F. (1968). Some theoretical considerations of bilingual development. *Psychological Bulletin, 70,* 647–670.

Ronjat, J. (1913). *Le development du langage observé chez un enfant bilingue.* Paris: Champion.

Sandoval-Martínez, S. (1982). Findings from the Head Start bilingual curriculum development and evaluation report. *NABE Journal, 7*(1), 1–12.

Schacter, F. F., Kirshner, D., Klips, B., Freidericks, M., & Sanders, K. (1974). Everyday preschool interpersonal speech usage: Methodological, development and sociolinguistic studies. *Monographs of Society for Research in Child Development.*

Skrabanek, R. L. (1970). Language maintenance among Mexican-Americans. *International Journal of Comparative Sociology, 11,* 272–282.

Smith, M. D. (1935). A study of the speech of eight bilingual children of the same family. *Child Development, 6,* 19–25.

Sorenson, A. P. (1967). Multilingualism in the Northwest Amazon. *American Anthropologist, 69,* 67–68.

Troike, R. C. (1981). Synthesis of research in bilingual education. *Educational Leadership, 38,* 498–504.

U.S. Commission on Civil Rights. (1974, February). Toward quality education for Mexican-Americans: Report 6. Mexican/American education study. Washington, DC: U.S. Commission on Civil Rights.

Williams, C. R. (1978). Early childhood education in the 1970's: Some reflections on reaching adulthood. *Teachers College Record, 79,* 529–538.

CHAPTER 3

Development, Values, and Knowledge in the Kindergarten Curriculum

Bernard Spodek

More and more children are attending kindergartens in public schools today than ever before. In addition, kindergarten is being seen as one area where the reform of public education can have a great impact. In order to optimize that impact, educators and public leaders are suggesting a variety of modifications of current kindergarten practice. Some are suggesting that the schedule of kindergarten classes be modified, with children attending kindergarten for a full school day, 5 days a week. Others are suggesting that children should have more than 1 year of kindergarten education — that public schools offer kindergarten to 4-year-olds as well as 5-year-olds. Still others are suggesting that the content of kindergarten education be modified, possibly providing academic instruction, normally reserved for grade 1 and beyond, to 5-year-olds and even 4-year-olds.

There is no clear consensus among educators or the general public on these suggestions. While some individuals argue for more academic instruction, there are others who argue that placing children in academic programs too early can damage their development. They worry that young children are being rushed through childhood and fear that children are being forced to face the demands of adulthood too soon. They decry the fact that children are being robbed of their childhood and denied the opportunity to engage in the natural activities of childhood — to be free and to play. Sometimes the argument tends toward the nostalgic, with an apparent longing for times when life was simpler and demands on children were fewer. But it has also been suggested that opportunities offered to young children for play and other expressive activities will, in the long run, lead to more positive outcomes in relation to intellectual and academic goals.

As a result of these varied suggestions, early childhood educators are being asked to appraise current kindergarten programs, to judge whether these programs are appropriate and effective. In making these appraisals, educators need to look beyond achievement data or the impressions of parents and teachers. The fundamental assumptions underlying these programs are being called into question, and these assumptions — basic conceptions of development and education as well as basic values related to children and society — need to be scrutinized.

There are many elements that go into the creation of an educational program for young children. Often, early childhood education programs have been viewed as extensions of our views of childhood. It sometimes seems to teachers that the curriculum can somehow be defined by carefully observing the child and finding out what the child needs to know and is interested in knowing. The suggestion has been made for a considerable time that early childhood programs be built to children's needs and interests. Children's interests, however, do not grow naturally from the child but rather are influenced by the social context in which the child functions. If a teacher shows interest in a topic and thus stimulates the child, that child will become interested in the same topic. Similarly, needs do not arise naturally but are related to elements that adults value. In either case, teachers are selective in their responses to children and will often ignore a felt need or expressed interest when it runs counter to their own values.

We need to explore all dimensions of the kindergarten curriculum if we are to determine whether it is adequate for children in today's society. We need to evaluate the curriculum from a developmental point of view, asking whether what we are teaching young children is developmentally appropriate. We need to evaluate it from a cultural context dimension, asking whether what we are teaching is worthwhile. Also, we need to evaluate it from a knowledge dimension, asking whether the way we are teaching children is consistent with the forms of knowledge taught, and thus can be tested by the child (Spodek, 1977). A look at all three of these dimensions of the kindergarten curriculum can provide us with the basis for determining an appropriate one for today's kindergarten.

THE DEVELOPMENTAL DIMENSION

Often early childhood programs have been viewed as selecting activities by following the cues that children provide. Johnson (1936/1970), for example, suggests that curriculum construction in the nursery school requires "an ordered analysis of observed behaviors; the outlining of stages and phases in development; and the conception of certain impulses and interests dominant in early childhood" (p. 6). Kindergarten curricula would be developed similarly. It is assumed that by knowing the needs and interests of young children and by understanding their capabilities in relation to their stage of development, one could design an appropriate program of education. Thus, a knowledge of child development was the basis for progressive early childhood education programs.

Similarly, most of the models of early childhood education that were developed since 1960 have been built upon conceptions of development although not strictly maturational, as noted above. Evans (1975) describes a number of programs that have been based upon specific developmental theories, some based upon behavioral theory, some based on Piagetian theory, and some on other developmental theories. The Educational Products Information Exchange has developed an analysis of early childhood educational programs that allows teachers to identify the developmental theory to which they subscribe and to then determine the educational program preferences that match that theory (Educational Products Information Exchange, 1972).

Such analyses suggest that educational programs for young children are rooted in one developmental theory or another. A number of early childhood educators, however, have suggested that developmental theory is not an appropriate foundation for early childhood educational programs. Fein and Schwartz (1982) made the distinction between developmental theories and educational theories, highlighting the limitations of using developmental theory as the basis for designing educational programs. They assert that theories of development are universalistic, describing the course of growth and change in sets of individuals. Because developmental theory addresses itself to broad trends in populations, it is of little use to educational practitioners who focus on what happens to particular individuals in specific settings. In addition, developmental theories are minimalist, identifying the core of minimum features in the environment that relate to growth and change. By contrast, educational theories are maximalist, concerned with the features of the environment that can cause the highest degrees of change and growth. These two forms of theory are not totally separable, however, since each type of theory informs the other.

Developmental theory might best be conceived of as a resource in developing kindergarten curriculum rather than as a source of curriculum. Developmental theory can help determine ways of testing the effectiveness of a program. It can also help determine the order in which activities might be presented and the level of developmental readiness necessary for children to achieve the goals of a program. Most important, it can become a tool for curriculum analysis (Spodek, 1973a).

THE CULTURAL CONTEXT DIMENSION

If we look closely at programs in early childhood education — both those that have operated in the past and those that exist today — we can identify many different purposes that have been served and continue to be served. When there is a consistency between the purposes served by the programs and the values of the society in which the programs operate, programs are popular and supported. As social values change, program goals and purposes are often modified, sometimes only subtly. As programs travel from community to community or from culture to culture, the programs are normally modified to make them more consistent with the values of the adopting society.

It is important to look at more than program effectiveness in evaluating a program. The worth of the program, its relation to the values of society, must also be addressed. A program that is effective, but whose goals are not consistent with societal values, may not be considered worthwhile.

Looking at Kindergartens in Historical Perspective

Kindergartens have existed in the United States for over 130 years. During this period, they have served a number of different purposes. They have been used to teach philosophical idealism, to "Americanize" children, to build proper habits, to provide emotional prophylaxis, to serve as a prelude to the elementary grades, to teach the content of school subjects, and to help develop "learning-how-to-learn" skills (Spodek, 1973b).

Friedrich Froebel founded the kindergarten in Germany in the first half of the nineteenth century. It was based upon a mystical religious philosophy concerning the unity of the individual, nature, God and other people. Froebel's original kindergarten was designed around a set of activities that allowed children to use his specifically created materials or "gifts." By using these graded materials, by involving children in arts and crafts activities or "occupations," and by having children sing the songs he wrote and play the games he prescribed, children were to gain access to the abstract ideas of the unity of the individual, God and nature. Each piece of equipment and each activity symbolized these ideas. The ideas were not presented directly to children, who would have had difficulty understanding these conceptualizations, but rather were offered to them through concrete symbolizations (Lilley, 1967).

As kindergartens were introduced into the United States, they were adopted by a variety of social agencies. In each case, the purpose of the agency was grafted on as programs were offered to specific populations of young children (Spodek, 1982). With the development of large urban centers and the influx of large numbers of immigrants from Europe, the kindergarten served as an institution to acculturate young children and their families. The children attended the kindergarten in the morning, and the kindergarten teachers worked with groups of mothers in the afternoon. These parents were taught proper child-rearing methods, American ways of buying, cooking, and serving food, ways to make proper items of clothing for the family, and skills in the use of the English language. Thus, the kindergarten served as a bridge to the American culture for both the children and their parents (Forest, 1927).

As progressive education took hold in America, its ideas helped to reform the kindergarten. Kindergarten activities were designed to reflect the experience of children growing up in contemporary American society. Under the influence of the behavioral psychologists, kindergartens focused on training young children to have proper habits. If proper habits were inculcated in young children, it was believed, their intellect would be improved. In addition, later education would not need to undo poor habits that might have been learned earlier by the children. The Conduct Curriculum developed at this time at Teachers College, Columbia University, provides an example of a kindergarten curriculum for habit training (Hill, 1923).

With the influence of the psychoanalytic movement on early childhood education, there was a shift from educating children for proper habits to helping children deal with emotional conflicts and providing them with opportunities to express their inner feelings. Dramatic play became important because it allowed children to play out conflict situations. Art and music activities served to provide children with forms of self-expression that were not dependent upon the use of written or spoken words. Teachers accepted a more indirect role in the classroom so as not to interfere with the children's needs for emotional catharsis (Headley, 1966).

During this period, kindergartens increasingly were becoming a part of public elementary schools. Elementary educators saw the kindergarten as an "educational halfway house," providing a bridge between home and school. Children learned to adapt to new rules and roles in the kindergarten. The kindergarten environment was more comfortable and secure than that of the other elementary classes, and the demands of the school could be tempered to the abilities of the children. Children could also be provided with the experiences and skills needed for success in the primary grades. The kindergarten provided a form of quality control for academic readiness. Although one could not predict the kinds of experiences that children would have at home, a set of common experiences could be offered in kindergarten. As a result of this common preparation, all children would be equally ready for the learning experiences provided in first grade.

In time the goal of kindergarten classes went beyond readiness. The more able children and the more ambitious teachers were challenged to grapple with the actual content of the primary grades in the year before the child entered them. With kindergartens becoming an almost universal part of the elementary school program, publishers extended their textbook series downward and included kindergarten materials along with their academic programs for grades 1–6. More and more children were having some early childhood educational experiences prior to their entering kindergarten, either in nursery schools or in day care centers. Fearful of boring children by having them simply repeat their preschool experiences, teachers began to offer elements of the elementary program in kindergarten as a way to provide more of a challenge to children (Spodek, 1982). In addition, newer theories of learning and development suggested that the early childhood years could be the most productive for intellectual development. Some enriched kindergarten programs focused precisely on well-defined intellectual skills, while other programs focused on more broadly defined "learning-how-to-learn" skills.

As we follow the progress of the kindergarten through the decades, we can see how its purposes and goals changed over time. Sometimes the philosophy of kindergarten education was modified as new knowledge about children's learning and development evolved. At other times new purposes were grafted onto the kindergarten without modifying the theory in any serious way. At all times kindergarten theory and contemporary social values influenced one another.

Looking at Contemporary Programs

An analysis of different contemporary early childhood programs similarly demonstrates how values related to work are projected into the curriculum in relation to programs' purposes. In Montessori programs, for example, the seriousness and spirituality of work is communicated through an atmosphere that teaches that work has its own internal rewards. In contrast, a 1975 description of Chinese kindergartens showed children participating in productive labor designed to communicate the social value of work (Kessen, 1975). The Behavior Analysis program developed at the University of Kansas (Bushell, 1973) describes children doing academic tasks in order to earn tokens used to "buy" desired activities. Here work was seen as a way to earn the opportunity to engage in personally satisfying activities. Traditional nursery-kindergarten classes have been viewed as a place where work is turned into games, thereby communicating to children that only those activities that are fun are worth doing (Spodek, 1977). In each case, either consciously or unconsciously, the early childhood curriculum was used to communicate social values about work to children.

Recently, in China, kindergarten children who were observed did not seem to be doing productive work. When I asked about this, the teachers explained that it was more important for the children to play. Thus, as the goals of that country have changed, it has become more important for children to engage in activities through which they might be expected to develop creative and expressive skills than for them to make an early contribution to the welfare of the community.

Kindergartens are responsive to the demands of new social structures, social values, and levels of technology. Dissatisfaction with kindergarten education may be a result of these programs' being out of phase with the surrounding cultural context, since there is always some lag in educational change. We must periodically reassess our programs and our purposes, reaffirming those purposes and values that we continue to hold while adapting programs to the new social demands and the new social requirements of kindergarten education.

THE KNOWLEDGE DIMENSION

All educational programs are concerned with imparting some form of knowledge to those who participate in them. This is as true for early childhood programs as for programs at higher levels of schooling. Often it seems that early childhood educators are less concerned about the knowledge we are imparting to young children than about other aspects of the programs, especially the programs' effect on children's development and the need to nurture children and provide for their basic care. Programs are described in relation to developmental principles rather than in relation to learning. Too often this obscures the fact that there are things that young children come to know as a result of participating in early childhood programs. What we want children to know affects what we teach them and, ultimately, what they learn. The valuing of different forms of knowledge in children leads to a valuing of different kinds of educational experiences provided to them. This can be illustrated by looking at historical approaches to early childhood education as well as at different contemporary programs.

Early Childhood Education in Colonial America

From the middle ages until about the 18th century, the Bible was seen as the source of knowledge in Western society. The content of the education in the primary schools was under the supervision of the community church. The test of the truth of a statement was determined by its consistency with biblical teachings. When, for example, Galileo (1564–1642) published his theories concerning the unity of principles of physics and astronomy, his text was rejected. It was not that his theories were inconsistent with observations made by physicists and astronomers. Rather, church officials saw the text as conflicting with the biblical descriptions of heaven and earth and therefore banned the book.

When the Bible is considered to be the only source of truth, then only literacy is needed to discover truth. If biblical meanings are to be interpreted for people, even this is not needed. However, in the Protestant tradition of the founders of the American colonies, each person was expected to discover his own interpretations of revealed truth by reading the Bible. Universal literacy became a goal, and schools were established.

In Puritan Massachusetts parents were admonished to teach their children to read as early as possible. Children as young as three attended the primary schools and often learned to read at age 3 or 4. Thus, no clear separation existed between preschool- and school-aged children, and, even well into the 19th century, a considerable proportion of children enrolled in the primary schools of the state were below the age of 5 (Kaestle & Vinovskis, 1978). The prime goal of Puritan schools was to teach reading to children, reflecting the religious purposes of such education. Even the secondary schools were religious in nature, designed to train clergymen and God-fearing leaders of the state (Noble, 1954).

In the early colonial period, the chief medium of instruction was the hornbook. This was a small sheet of paper or parchment on which the alphabet, prayers, benedictions, and religious admonitions were printed or written. This sheet was tacked to a paddle-shaped piece of wood, then covered with a thin layer of transparent horn. Children would learn the letters of the alphabet from the hornbook, then they would learn to sound out the consonants, each followed by a vowel. When they could sound out all the combinations, they went on to sound out words. Once the hornbook was mastered, the children read from the Bible or from some other religious text.

A new medium of instruction, *The New England Primer*, was published in the last decade of the 17th century. This remained in use for over 100 years. This primer included an illustrated alphabet and a set of rhymes as well as a short catechism and religious admonitions. Even the rhymes had a religious and moral tone, as noted in the ones illustrating the first two letters of the alphabet:

> In Adam's Fall,
> We sinned all.
>
> Thy Life to mend,
> This Book attend.

The first school for many of these children was a dame's school. Such schools might be held in the cramped kitchen or bedroom of a housewife — generally a widow — who served as the teacher. Women who ran these schools often had no background in language learning or educational methodology. The small fee they collected might be their only means of support (Good & Teller, 1973).

More formal schools were also established during this period. In 1647 the general court of Massachusetts passed what was to be called the "old deluder Satan" law, which required all towns with 50 or more families to maintain an elementary school and those with 100 or more families to establish a secondary school as well. (Education was seen as the way to save the populace from the devil.) Not every community followed the law, and often, when schools were established, they operated for only a few months a year. Thus, the education that colonial American children received was meager, though significantly more than was offered to most children in the world at that time.

These colonial schools were consistent with the view of knowledge held by the communities that supported them: The Bible was the source of all knowledge. As American society became more secular and as other forms of knowledge came to be valued, the school curriculum expanded, first with the inclusion of writing and arithmetic, but later with the addition of studies in other areas of knowledge as well.

Nineteenth- and Twentieth-Century Early Childhood Programs

The latter part of the 18th century has been called the Age of Reason. During this period of enlightenment, other sources of knowledge besides religious dogma came to be recognized. Rationalism and empiricism evolved as significant concepts of knowledge. Not only did these theories arouse philosophical discourse, they also influenced the development of early childhood educational programs.

Empiricism is the belief that sense perceptions play a central role in the generation and validation of knowledge. We gather information through our experience, which is internalized through the senses. The more experience we have, the more information we can accumulate. Under the influence of empiricism, observation and experimentation became the basis for scientific knowledge. Truth was tested empirically by way of experience, and generalizations were seen as the result of the accumulation of consistent experience.

While Robert Owen's original Infant School is usually viewed as a reflection of a particular social philosophy, it also reflected an educational philosophy based upon empiricism. According to Owen, knowledge is derived from the objects surrounding the individual, and truth is defined as what is consistent with nature. Both are basic empirical assumptions. Reading continued to play a central role in Owen's Infant School, but children were also taught through experience about the animal, vegetable, and mineral world. Children would leave the classroom to make observations from nature, and geographic and zoological specimens were provided for children to observe with the classroom (Owen, 1824).

Froebel's kindergarten contrasts with this approach and represents a rationalist view of education. Rationalism posits that truths are composed of self-evident premises. These premises are not derived from experience but are held to be logical and undeniably true. Logical conclusions are believed to be statements of fact about the world. Mathematics is an example of a field of knowledge based upon a system of rational thought. Mathematical facts are logically derived rather than empirically developed.

Froebel's educational program was based upon a set of key ideas that were considered to be basic to an understanding of the world (Froebel, 1887). Central to this was the idea of the unity of individual, God, and nature. Each person, for example, mirrors in some sense the whole to which he or she belongs, while at the same time being a unique individual. This was Froebel's notion of *Gliedganzes*. Froebel's kindergarten was designed to communicate these basic ideas about the unity of the world to young children through a set of activities and materials that symbolized them. Children in this program were not taught to test reality through contact with these materials, but rather to learn the self-evident truths that were expressed by the materials.

The first *gift* in a Froebelian kindergarten was a set of balls. These educational materials were given to children, not to help them learn about the nature of spherical objects, but to symbolize for them the unity of the world. The child was then given a cube, whose six sides represented diversity. Finally, the child was given a cylinder. The cylinder is a three-dimensional form that has some elements of both the sphere and the cube. The cylinder was used to represent the mediation of opposites.

The arguments that Froebelian kindergarten educators had with progressive kindergarteners at the turn of the 20th century were not related to program effectiveness, but to the *meaning of experience*. Since the Froebelians were not empiricists, they put no stock in the direct observations of children or in educational experimentation. Thus, the two camps of early childhood educators could find no middle ground of agreement regarding the education of young children, since each rejected the other's source of knowledge.

The Montessori method represents a more systematic approach to empirically oriented education than was found in Robert Owen's Infant School. Maria Montessori (1870–1952) created a form of education to train the senses so that individuals could perceive the world more sensitively and so that they could order their perceptions more methodically. In the Montessori school children are provided with sensory training through a set of materials that isolate particular attributes of experience. This allows children to focus on particular aspects of sensation and learn how to order them. Some materials might lead the children to focus on size, for example, with no attention given to other attributes. Other materials similarly focus on color, and still other materials will focus on shape or weight.

While rationalism allows individuals to understand some aspects of intellectual knowledge, empiricism allows individuals to understand other aspects of knowledge. Neither approach alone can account for the sum total of intellectual knowledge, and each approach alone is an inadequate tool for understanding the world. While we observe the world directly to obtain information, there are no naturally occurring ways of ordering that information. We create an orderly world that allows us to ascribe meaning to our perceptions. For example, we do not perceive causality. We infer causality, believing that an incident that occurs first is the cause of a later incident. We develop generalizations about the world based on the consistency of our experience, but we have to create those generalizations. This requires an assumption that what has consistently occurred in the past will continue to occur in the future. Given this conception of how we come to know the world, we would find that neither sharp observation nor skillful use of logic is enough to understand the world*.

---

*In developing my position on causation, I am aware that others, particularly philosophers such as David Hume, for example, have discussed this concept before. Their work has had a strong influence on my thinking.

Over the past three decades a number of early childhood education programs that have been developed have built upon the work of the developmental epistemologist Jean Piaget. Although these programs differ from one another in significant ways, there is common agreement regarding the nature of knowledge and its relationships to experience in young children (Forman & Fosnot, 1982).

From a Piagetian perspective, knowledge is more than the accumulation and ordering of experience or the search for self-evident truths. Each individual constructs knowledge through the application of logical thinking. Individuals use the information gained from experience as a data base and as a source of validation. This knowledge takes the form of conceptual systems or schemata that are continually being tested against experience to be affirmed, elaborated, modified, or discarded. Children are given a wide and rich set of experiences in these programs. They are also given the opportunity to make sense of the world and to create knowledge by acting upon the information they gather.

Teachers play an active role in such programs. Not only do they plan experiences that match the intellectual capabilities of the children in their classes, but they also provide experiences that mismatch the children's intellectual capabilities by presenting problems to be solved or complicating the children's world so that they must come up with more sophisticated ways of viewing and understanding that world. Teachers must also create social environments in which children can test their understanding of the world against one another without too great an emotional risk. Such a form of education must be open-ended to some extent, with the teacher having a sense of the goals that children should achieve. At the same time teachers must follow the leads of children, being aware of what they do not understand well and what they do understand. Such an approach to early childhood education can never be prepackaged.

The theories discussed here relate to cognitive knowlege. Each is concerned with developing statements that reflect reality, and each identifies ways of testing the truth of these statements. There are other forms of knowledge, however, that are equally valid but that may not necessarily be concerned with determining objective reality. Some may not even be concerned with knowledge that can be articulated in words. The skills that a sportsman displays or that a craftsman has are also valid forms of knowledge. These skills, however, may only be manifested in an act or in a product. Thus, in playing a game of tennis, knowledge is displayed that is quite different from that shown in describing the game. In creating a vase an artisan may express more of what is known about the nature of shape and form, the qualities of clay, and the potential of a set of tools and a potters' wheel than can ever be expressed in a description of that vase or of the process of creating the vase.

Similarly, good medical diagnosticians seem to know more than can be objectively determined from a set of medical tests, and good psychotherapists have a sense of what is happening to their patients which goes beyond what is heard in a transcript of the therapeutic session. Animal lovers who are adept at handling a particular breed of animal, or individuals who seem to know how to deal with every social crisis, may also possess a form of nondiscursive knowledge that can only partially be described in words and may not be capable of objective description or validation. Polanyi (1958) talks about forms of personal knowledge that go beyond the cognitive. Phenix (1964) has described a broad range of knowledge that he has categorized into six realms of meaning: *symbolics*, including language, mathematics, and nondiscursive symbolic forms; *empirics*, which are matters of fact derived from experience; *aesthetics*, including the arts; *synnoetics*, which results from meditation or reflection; *ethics*, which express obligation; and *synoptics*, which are comprehensively integrative forms of knowledge.

In each society and in each era, communities decide which areas of knowledge should be taught by the schools. The issues of whether the schools should be concerned with general knowledge or whether they should be vocationally oriented, whether they should deal with narrow concerns or whether they should respond to the whole child, whether they should include sex education, or religious training, or an understanding of multicultural perspectives — all these issues relate to which areas of knowledge should be the domain of the school. We limit what the schools teach, since there are many other educational institutions in society, including families, religious institutions, the work place, and the armed forces. These other institutions also have a responsibility for education that is related to some particular domain of knowledge. In addition, no society requires that children know everything. The issue of when a particular area of knowledge should be taught, along with what should be taught, also affects early childhood education.

At different times, we have included different forms of knowledge in our early childhood education programs. The influence of psychoanalytic theory on the progressive kindergartens of the 1920s and 1930s was an expression of concern for teaching children something more than academics or cognitive knowledge. Children were helped to understand that their inner feelings and their relationships with others were legitimate forms of knowledge. They could gain greater understandings of these through dramatic play. They used a variety of art media to communicate knowledge they could not express in words. Social interaction was nurtured as a way of validating some forms of knowledge that could not be objectively validated.

Some of the concerns that are voiced about program evaluation reflect a feeling that programs may be teaching one form of knowledge but may be evaluated in relation to children's achieving other forms of knowledge. Teachers fear that their attempts to teach creativity, problem solving, or social competence are distorted when the children they teach do not do well on tests of academic readiness. Yet we find few valid and reliable measures that allow us to assess children's learning outside the realm of academics. The arguments heard after the evaluation of the various curriculum models that were part of the Follow Through program voiced this concern. Many project sponsors felt they were improperly evaluated, since the goals of their programs, the forms of knowledge they wished to have children learn, were not properly assessed. In the quest for program effectiveness and the limitations we have on what areas of knowledge we can assess, program goals and curriculum can easily become distorted (House, Glass, McLean, & Walker, 1978).

REFLECTING ON TODAY'S KINDERGARTEN CURRICULUM

There have been many changes in society since kindergartens were first introduced into the United States 130 years ago. As these changes have taken place, kindergarten programs have also changed. Like all educational programs, the kindergarten has continually been modified to reflect what we know about children — how they learn and how they develop. Kindergartens have also been modified to reflect changing cultural values and cultural demands. Some of the early changes were related to the urbanization of our population and its movement into cities. More recently we have seen attempts to change programs in relation to changing concepts of the roles of men and women, changing levels of technology, and changing forms of communication. Radio, television, and computers have all influenced our kindergartens. In addition, as we have come to know more about how we come to know what we know, we have been required to modify our curriculum and our ways of teaching to help children become more knowledgeable.

If the kindergarten is to remain a vital and dynamic educational institution serving children and communities, early childhood educators will need to assess and reassess what we do with young children in kindergarten. Through this assessment we may confirm that what we have been doing remains educationally sound. We may also find that we will need to expand, revise, and modify our approaches to educating young children. We may even wish to substitute new activities for traditional ones so that our kindergartens can help children become more knowledgeable and so that our programs can become even more developmentally appropriate while responding to the needs and values of our society.

REFERENCES

Bushell, D. (1973). The behavior analysis classroom. In B. Spodek (Ed.), *Early childhood education* (pp. 163–175). Englewood Cliffs, NJ: Prentice-Hall.

Educational Products Information Exchange (1972). *Early childhood education: How to select and evaluate programs.* New York: EPIE Institute.

Evans, E. D. (1975). *Contemporary influences in early childhood education.* New York: Holt, Rinehart and Winston.

Fein, G., & Schwartz, P. M. (1982). Developmental theories in early education. In B. Spodek (Ed.), *Handbook of research in early childhood education* (pp. 82–104). New York: Free Press.

Forest, I. (1927). *Preschool education.* New York: Macmillan.

Forman, G. E., & Fosnot, C. T. (1982). The use of Piaget's constructivism in early childhood education programs. In B. Spodek (Ed.), *Handbook of research in early childhood education* (pp. 185–211). New York: Free Press.

Froebel, F. (1887). *The education of man.* (W. N. Hailmann, Trans.). New York: Appleton.

Good, H. G., & Teller, J. D. (1973). *A history of American education* (3rd ed.). New York: Macmillan.

Headley, N. (1966). *Foster and Headley's education in the kindergarten* (4th ed.). New York: American Book Co.

Hill, P. S. (1923). *A conduct curriculum for the kindergarten and first grade.* New York: Scribners.

House, E. R., Glass, G. V., McLean, L. D., & Walker, D. F. (1978). No simple answer: Critique of follow through evaluation. *Harvard Educational Review, 48,* 128–162.

Johnson, H. (1970). *Schools begin at two.* New York: Agathon Press (first published in 1936).

Kaestle, C. F., & Vinovskis, M. A. (1978). From apron strings to ABC's: Parents, children and schooling in nineteenth century Massachusetts. In J. Demos & S. S. Boocock (Eds.), *Turning points: Historical and sociological essays on the family* (pp. 39–80). Chicago: University of Chicago Press.

Kessen, W. (1975). *Childhood in China.* New Haven: Yale University Press.

Lilley, I. M. (1967). *Friedrich Froebel: A selection from his writings.* Cambridge: Cambridge University Press.

Noble, S. G. (1954). *A history of American education* (Rev. ed.). New York: Rinehart and Co.

Owen, R. D. (1824). *Outline of a system of education at New Lanark.* Glasgow: Wardlaw and Cunningham.

Phenix, P. (1964). *Realms of meaning.* New York: McGraw-Hill.

Polanyi, M. (1958). *Personal knowledge.* Chicago: University of Chicago Press.

Spodek, B. (1973a). *Early childhood education*. Englewood Cliffs, NJ: Prentice-Hall.

Spodek, B. (1973b). Needed: A new view of kindergarten education. *Childhood Education, 40*(5), 191–197.

Spodek, B. (1977). What constituted worthwhile educational experiences for young children? In B. Spodek (Ed.), *Teaching practices: Reexamining assumptions* (pp. 5–20). Washington, DC: National Association for the Education of Young Children.

Spodek, B. (1982). The kindergarten: A retrospective and contemporary view. In B. Spodek (Ed.), *Current topics in early childhood education: Vol. 4* (pp. 173–191). Norwood, NJ: Ablex.

Spodek, B. (1985). Early childhood education's past as prologue. *Young Children, 40*(5), 3–7.

CHAPTER 4

.ndergarten Reading: A Proposal for a Problem-Solving Approach

Jana M. Mason

In a small rural midwestern elementary school, the kindergarten children file in, hang up their coats, and collect their cigar boxes of pencils, crayons, and small treasures from a shelf. There are no toys and few books on the shelves, and the boxed games and puzzles are not pulled out. No art or science areas have been set up in the room; the housekeeping corner, a sparsely furnished place, is seldom used. Children ignore the neatly displayed pictures that they have colored or cut and pasted from shapes drawn by the teacher or from commercial materials. Instead, they move their boxes of belongings to one of the five tables in the room, each of which has six small chairs, and sit down at their designated places. Few talk to their neighbors, and, curiously, no one begins to work, read, or write. Some put their heads on the table. Others look in their boxes or at other children, waiting for the school day to begin.

As the bell breaks the silence, the teacher gets up from her desk and leads the children in the pledge of allegiance, roll call, and the introduction of the reading lesson. The lesson, on words that begin with the letter T, takes 45 minutes. Everyone takes part in the same lesson, first by listening and singing along softly to the "Letter T" song. Next they answer the teacher's questions, calling out and raising their hands; then they fill out the worksheets that go with the commercially produced lesson. The teacher walks the aisles, helping if children make errors and redirecting those that do not stay on task. While the attention of a few children strays, no one misbehaves or appears unhappy. Most of the children are eager to participate in the activity and listen seriously to the teacher's questions and directions for work. They are learning to read, they know they are learning, and they seem to appreciate the opportunity.

In a university community, a busing program in the district draws kindergarten children from low-income and professional families to the same school. As children enter and hang up their coats, they choose from

48

a wide range of activities. The room is crowded with shelves of materials. There are a housekeeping center, blocks and painting areas, a science table, and several locations for books, puzzles, and games. Children's artwork decorates the walls. Some children come in with books in their hands, others with toys. They group with their friends on the jungle gym, build a block structure, set up a dramatic play activity in a separate small playroom, or sit on the rug, looking at a book or reading alone or with another child. The free-choice play activity continues uninterrupted for 15 or 20 minutes.

No bell announces the beginning of the school day; no formal roll is called; the teacher has not directed the whole class to begin working, but lessons have begun. The teacher has been listening to a child read and is asking questions about the story. She sits at a child-sized table and calls children over individually to read to her, then hands out and explains math and phonics worksheet exercises and points out an exploratory science activity for them to do. As they are called on to read and are given assignments, the children shift from their chosen activity to working on math, science, and reading. There are no assigned places. Some children choose a place alone, while most sit with friends. There they ask help from one another and talk quietly about the work and other activities. When they finish the assignments, they go to the rug with a book and read. Many help one another or read together. They seem to be integrating reading and writing into their everyday activities; reading does not stand out as a separate subject. After an hour or longer, the teacher calls them together for group activities such as marking the calendar and weather for the day, story reading, and show-and-tell discussion.

In these two classrooms reading is successfully taught, but with very dissimilar approaches. Observations in kindergartens such as these show that reading instruction can be a part of the program, and research shows positive effects from some programs, particularly those for low-income children. Kindergarten children seem ready to learn and able to profit from letter-recognition, reading, and writing activities. There are, however, major differences in the way kindergarten reading programs are structured. These differences, which are not trivial, affect more than children's reading behavior.

Why are there such disparate reading programs in kindergarten? One reason is that literacy standards are undergoing a change, a situation that leads to the consideration of new instructional ideas. Another reason is a lack of agreement about how children ought to be taught. Current developmental and cognitive theories are just now being interpreted and tried out, but few as yet have affected practice. Since most kindergarten teachers were schooled to follow earlier constructs about learning and since community attitudes about how to teach young children, which are also influential, reflect parents' own childhood experiences, earlier views still have a hold on reading practice.

Changes in literacy standards are described in the next section, followed by a description of theoretical changes in learning that have guided kindergarten reading instruction for the last two decades. Earlier theories focused either on maturation or on experience, while current work utilizes a problem-solving construct.

HISTORICAL CHANGES IN LITERACY

Literacy in the 17th and 18th centuries was not widespread. Records kept in parishes in Sweden, one of the countries that were literate, according to Resnick and Resnick (1977), showed that though most people could read, literacy was at a low level. Reading, reciting, and recall of religious material was typically all that was required. In the 19th century, Resnick and Resnick report, as education for children began to be compulsory, history and geography texts that cultivated love of the familiar and exalted patriotism were included in the reading curriculum. But this did not necessarily lead to wide reading because, according to Smith (1965), oral recitation of familiar written passages, rather than reading new and unfamiliar material, was stressed.

Educational testing of U.S. Army recruits during World War I helped change reading practice and literacy standards. These tests uncovered the fact that nearly 30% of the recruits could not write a simple letter or read a newspaper even though most had attended public school. These revelations led to better educational evaluation techniques and to a requirement that literacy should mean an ability to read and understand unfamiliar texts as well as familiar ones.

Literacy standards continue to be a function of changes in social needs. Today, people are being asked to go beyond leisure reading of unfamiliar texts. With the increased demands of technology, more reading is needed as part of one's work, and an ability to analyze texts and read critically is expected. Presuming widespread literacy is not abandoned, this shift to higher literacy standards will force changes in reading instruction practices. Different reading instructional approaches will undoubtedly be required, even in kindergarten.

Coincidental with changes in literacy standards has been the development of different theories about learning. Currently there is a renewed emphasis on comprehension and critical reading; story reading, listening comprehension, and learning to write as well as to read are being stressed. Reviews by Mason (1985), and Teale and Sulzby (1986), suggest how earlier instructional practices were related to early reading practice. Learning to read was explained in terms of a maturational construct and then according to skill-based instruction principles. Reviews by Wagoner (1983) and Reeve and Brown (1984) describe the emerging current problem-solving perspective.

MATURATION AND READING READINESS

A maturationist view of reading development was proposed in the 1920s and 1930s based on the notion that reading skill development, like motor development, was a function of neural ripening, a genetically programmed unfolding. There was thought to be an optimum period before which instruction was fruitless, if not harmful. The theory was supported by work on twins (e.g., McGraw, 1935) that purported to show that instruction in a skill before the appropriate period was less effective than instruction provided when the child displayed an interest in the activity.

Morphett and Washburne (1931), who accepted this view, attempted to determine the optimum time for learning to read. In a comparison of children's IQ scores at the beginning of first grade with their February and June progress in reading, they found that children with a mental age of 6.5 or above made better progress. Even though this study was later criticized (e.g., Gates & Bond, 1936), and reanalyses showed overinterpretation of the original twin studies (e.g., Hunt, 1983), the construct of readiness was retained.

A key element of the maturational perspective has been the delay of reading instruction until children expressed a readiness to learn. Until fairly recently, then, parents were admonished not to teach their children to read before they went to school. Kindergarten teachers were trained to organize instruction around more general social, motor, and cognitive constructs and advised not to teach reading. Children were to become "ready" for reading by coloring and cutting on the line, copying shapes, and matching pictures. They learned to recognize numerals and count and to name letters, but words, including common sign and label words, were not taught. Story listening was recommended, but story reading, even if it occurred by memorizing and reciting the text, was discouraged.

Reading instruction was to be delayed until children were mature enough to listen to, follow, and learn with formal instruction. This was thought to occur at about age six. It was furthermore argued that those children who failed to learn to read in first grade had been slow to mature and thus not ready to learn.

The notion of delaying instruction until children are ready is still evident. Parents may be told to keep their child out of kindergarten for another year because the child acts immaturely, has motor or coordination problems, has low readiness test scores, or is somewhat younger than the others in the class. Some kindergarten teachers exclude low-scoring children from the regular program of instruction. Unfortunately, besides learning that they are somehow not as good as the other children, they are probably also learning how to tune out the teacher. Although these may be the children most in need of opportunities to print, look at books, and recognize letters and words, they are not learning how to talk about and use printed information.

SKILL LEARNING

According to Durkin (1968), the emphasis on maturation and an unfolding readiness to learn began to change in the 1960s. In its place came a belief that experiences with well-organized tasks were the key to effective reading instruction, even for young children. It was proposed that the influences of maturation could be counteracted if learning materials and tasks were appropriately sequenced from easy to difficult, using small increments, and with guided practice at each step. Instructional materials were to highlight these learning principles. Thus, instruction began to emphasize the role of environmental factors over developmental factors.

This instructional shift took place when research (e.g., Bloom, 1956; Skinner, 1953; Bruner, Goodnow, & Austin, 1956) was beginning to show that what tasks are given and in what order they are given make a difference in learning. It was assumed that "most students can attain a high level of learning capacity if instruction is approached sensitively and systematically, if students are helped when and where they have learning difficulty, if they are given sufficient time to achieve mastery, and if there is some clear criterion of what constitutes mastery" (Bloom, 1976, p. 4).

Reading activities were organized into sets of skills, taught in a particular order, and measured in terms of attainment or mastery of the skills. These were organized as reading readiness tasks, thus utilizing one part of the maturational concept, that of preparing children for reading. Reading readiness tasks reflecting this outlook are part of most commercial materials for kindergarten. These materials typically feature stepwise exercises in picture matching, picture sequencing, letter recognition, letter tracing, and copying.

Such reading readiness tasks have become the principle content of kindergarten reading. It is assumed that they *prepare* children for reading using visual orientation and discrimination tasks, teaching letter identification, and acquainting children with a few of the words to appear in the first-grade textbooks. Word or story reading is seldom taught. For example, one popular 1983 basal program has pictures with no words or letters on about half of the children's pages, pictures with letters on a quarter, and words with letters or pictures on the remaining quarter. No pages have words alone. Tasks on the picture pages include discrimination of colors or shapes and left-right progression tasks. Pages with letters and pictures together are intended to help children match letter names with objects that begin with the letter. Word pages usually involve a copying or tracing task. However, most of the words are not a required part of this program. Learning words and letter sounds are an optional instructional step taught in first grade.

Programs such as this one reflect a skill-based perspective with activities and tasks hierarchically ordered by difficulty. For example, letter names and their visual discrimination are taught before sounds and the words in which they appear. Also, few comprehension skills are taught, because letters and some sight words are thought to be needed first.

Instruction is these programs is organized by presenting a skill, followed by practice materials that are arranged in terms of word and sentence difficulty. For example, a typical lesson, meant to teach children to identify letters, directs them to the upper- and lowercase forms of the letter on the page and asks for the name. Next they look at the picture, which contains several examples of objects that begin with the letter. The children are told the names of the objects and that those words begin with the letter being studied. A practice exercise follows in which children are to listen to the name of the picture and circle the letter that fits. Flaws in this lesson include the following: no opportunity for children to think of words beginning with the letter or for the teacher to assess their understanding of the letter-sound-to-word connection; and practice materials that do not adequately test the concepts.

PROBLEM SOLVING

An alternative perspective draws on the notion of reading as a thinking and understanding act and learning to read as a constructive, problem-solving process. This means, for example, that while children can be given information to learn and practice in a stepwise fashion, they must interpret the ideas and relate them to their own knowledge and experience. They must monitor their understanding and put together their own underlying structure of the information. In so doing, children's own thinking strategies about how to approach, learn about, and remember printed information become the focus of both the reading process and its instruction.

Effective older readers oversee their comprehension and guide their thinking and learning using appropriate reading and memory strategies. According to Reeve and Brown (1984), this idea is long-standing in psychology (consider the 1890 monograph of James). It was rediscovered by Flavell (1981), who realized that young children were not using appropriate memory strategies, though they could do so if reminded. The children lacked *knowledge about memory processes*, principally, knowing how to reflect about the process of memorizing information and having conscious control of its operation. These abilities, however, are found in older children who are good readers.

Viewing reading as a problem-solving activity and having conscious control of one's thoughts as one reads are referred to as comprehension monitoring. This is the ability to regulate and watch over one's comprehension while reading. For example, to set appropriate reading goals and plan how to read a text, a reader should know where the most important or most interesting information in the text is located and how to search for it. Realizing when one has stopped comprehending and knowing how to choose and apply appropriate fix-up strategies when one does not understand are also critical.

While it is clear that comprehension monitoring is a component of successful reading, its links to preschool reading and language experiences and to kindergarten reading instruction have seldom been considered. Next are five tasks in which research has shown an effect of comprehension monitoring. Each is briefly described and then related to kindergarten instruction.

Listening Comprehension and Production Tasks

Young children (5- to 7-year-olds) have difficulty differentiating inadequate messages from those that contain enough information (Markman, 1979) or from constructing complete messages (Robinson & Robinson, 1976). Flavell (1981) reported that the problems of younger children in detecting inadequate messages could be due to a willingness to adopt a less exact criterion. In the face of uncertainty, younger children accept closure too readily. This suggests that story listening activities, for example, should be followed by opportunities for kindergarten children to act out the important story events so that they can see the related pieces of texts and find occasions when the text is too limited.

Reading Comprehension Tasks

Younger and low-performing readers are less likely to detect text comprehension problems than are older, effective readers (Canney & Winograd, 1979; Markman, 1981). Moreover, they are less able to pick out difficult-to-remember stories (Owings, Peterson, Bransford, Morris, & Stein, 1980), more likely to focus on hard words rather than inconsistent information as being the cause of incomprehensible text (Garner, 1980, 1981), and less able to identify and correct anomaly and nongrammaticality in sentences and judge and clarify ambiguity in reading, listening, or writing (Menyuk, 1984). Menyuk suggested that young and low-performing readers lack a broad base of linguistic knowledge. Discussion of story meaning in kindergarten ought to help prepare children for attention to the text meaning rather than to the words, letters, or pictures.

Protocol Analyses

Readers can be asked to read aloud, stopping at predetermined points to tell what they are thinking about. The ability to discuss their reading problems and strategies is related to reading ability (Hare, 1981). Good but not poor readers use the following strategies: reading for meaning, rereading, selective reading, and adjusting reading speed (Hare & Pulliam, 1980). To help children develop these strategies in kindergarten, teachers might introduce children to poems, articles, and informational reports as well as to stories and discuss how to put on different "listening ears" for different texts.

Interview Studies

Meyers and Paris (1978) found that older children are able to describe strategies for resolving comprehension failure. Younger and poor readers describe monitoring strategies and use decoding-oriented rather than meaning-oriented strategies (Paris & Meyers, 1981; Thomas, 1980). Also, poor readers are absorbed in their own status as learners instead of focusing on comprehension (Fischer & Mandl, 1982). A possible antidote is for kindergarten teachers to encourage children to talk about being confused by a story they hear and what they might do to understand it.

Reading Performance Tasks

DiVesta, Hayward, and Orlando (1979) found that poor readers are less likely to use appropriate look-ahead strategies to carry out a cloze task. Garner and Alexander (1982) found that students who use a question-predicting strategy without prompting outperform students who do not use the strategy. The research suggests that while kindergarten teachers are reading stories to children they can stop and ask for predictions about what might happen next.

A *problem-solving* approach can be initiated in kindergarten to help children reflect on their knowledge, to oversee and guide their thinking, to plan, regulate, or monitor, and check their listening comprehension. Problem-solving activities might reduce the differences later between good and poor readers' ability to express and apply effective reading comprehension strategies. They should reduce the tendency to misidentify hard-to-read and flawed texts, to choose inappropriate and inadequate strategies, or to leap too quickly to resolution of text meaning.

LITERACY LEARNING AS A PROBLEM-SOLVING VENTURE

There are other, more generally stated theoretical constructs about problem solving, derived principally from work on formal operational thought (Inhelder & Piaget, 1958). Siegler (1978), for example, describes how problem solving can be understood as an attitude or mode of thinking. It involves the ability "to reason both inductively and deductively, to consider all possible outcomes, and to recognize and admit when the evidence is insufficient to reach any conclusion. . . . Two conditions are thought to be crucial. One is thorough familiarity with the old way of doing things, either concrete operations or the established paradigm. The other is frequent encounters with problems in which the existing framework is clearly inadequate, problems in which the usual approach either yields no answers or incorrect ones" (p. 110).

To learn to read can be thought of as a problem-solving venture. For beginning readers, for example, a principal problem is recognition and recall of printed words. Children try out word recognition approaches, usually looking at the initial letter, then at most consonants, and then at the vowel with the consonants (Mason, 1976). The use of increasingly more sophisticated strategies reflects more advanced knowledge about words and letter sounds. The ability to apply more appropriate word recognition strategies, however, requires great familiarity with print and an ability to realize that an old conceptual framework is not adequate. A kindergarten program that features printed information in context and encourages children to figure out ways to remember the words should lead to effective problem-solving tools for recognizing, understanding, and remembering printed information.

LANGUAGE ANALYSIS AS A VEHICLE FOR LITERACY

Children who begin thinking analytically by talking about their language learn that language is not merely a way to convey oral information. According to Olson (1984), it leads to a different way of thinking and reasoning. Language then becomes a structure that can be studied, analyzed, and interpreted.

An analytic treatment of language is apparently fostered by middle-class parents. For example, Snow and Ninio (1986) show that mothers play a "naming game" when reading picture books to young children. Schieffelin and Cochran-Smith (1984) describe how storybooks are used by middle-class American parents not only to entertain but "as a way to initiate problem-solving discussions [and] a way to verify and introduce new information" (p. 6). Heath (1983) describes differences between middle- and low-income families' discussions with their children. Middle-income parents teach their children how to discuss events, answer questions, and structure their discussions with others. Low-income parents often do not.

Olson argues that deliberate language instruction is an important antecedent to literacy because it leads to an analytic orientation toward reading. He suggests that children learn a set of concepts for referring to language. They have opportunities to express these concepts using explicit metalinguistic nouns such as *word, sentence,* and *letter;* metalinguistic verbs such as *say, ask, assert,* and *request;* and metacognitive verbs such as *believe, desire, intend, mean, think, pretend, wonder, decide, realize, remember,* and *doubt.* The metalanguage becomes a medium through which children can refer to and think about written language structures and meaning.

Literacy and Language Development

Wells (1981) proposes three major phases of linguistic development. His third phase is similar to Olson's notion that language becomes an analytic tool. His three phases are:

1. *Discovery of language,* in which patterns of sound take on meaning and purpose and language represents or stands for objects and events.
2. *Consolidation and diversification,* in which acquisition of speaking, listening, and language-interpreting conventions are tuned to the required social contexts.
3. *Detachment from immediate context,* in which one is conscious

of one's own mental states and able to reflect on one's own experience, to separate thought and action, and to separate language
from its context.

Wells argues that the alphabetic writing system led to the "ability
to abstract linguistic expressions from the particular content and contexts
to which they initally referred . . . [so] with the acquisition of literacy
comes a more detached and reflective attitude to experience and this, in
turn, promotes higher levels of cognitive functioning than are readily
available in cultures that are restricted to purely oral communication"
(p. 243).

A similar point was made by Elsasser and John-Steiner (1977), who
considered how the elaboration of inner thought is developed into its written form by learning to move from compact inner speech, through which
experiences are stored, to the details and deliberations of a comprehen-
sible written form. Using written language requires the person to develop
a sense of personal control of language, eventually reaching a desire and
need for educationally transmitted knowledge.

KINDERGARTEN IMPLICATIONS

A kindergarten curriculum can promote literacy in conjunction with
the development of problem-solving abilities. Problem solving can foster
a use of word-recognition and comprehension-monitoring strategies. It
can begin before children have learned to read, such as through discussion and acting out of written material, and can act as a guiding principle while learning to read. Given a problem-solving orientation from the
start, children may form the habit of looking for familiar letter patterns
and meaningful information as they read. However, learning to treat
reading as an active, constructive process is likely to be more effective
in a literacy-rich classroom environment with a program of activities that
give children the opportunity to talk about, listen to, read, write, and
remember printed information. In this way reading, writing, and speaking become fully integrated and better related to their experiences at home
and in the community.

Guidelines for establishing a kindergarten reading program are represented as three principles (Mason & Au, 1986): *a literacy-rich classroom,
a multifaceted program*, and *active processing*. They are based on observation of successful kindergarten reading programs (Mason, Stewart, &
Dunning, 1986), analysis of story-reading lessons (Dunning & Mason,

1984; Peterman, Dunning & Mason, 1985; Mason, McCormick & Bhavnagri, 1983), and tryouts of reading materials with children in Head Start and kindergarten classrooms (Mason & Au, 1984; McCormick & Mason, 1984).

Maintain a Literacy-Rich Environment

Learning to read is supported when a classroom features familiar printed information and interesting literacy activities. Children's pictures can be on the walls, and paper and art supplies, as well as spaces for children's coats, can be labeled. There should be easily accessible books placed in a comfortable and quiet place. Alphabet posters, letter and word games, and other literacy-related games should be available. Time must be provided to use printed materials, and such use should be part of many different classroom activities. The classroom environment should support literacy and serve as a bridge between home experiences and the more demanding work of first grade.

Children can be provided a literacy-rich environment, given opportunities to listen to and discuss written information, and offered the chance to figure out how words are written, pronounced, and used meaningfully in sentences and stories. Developing literacy in a supportive fashion with familiar materials and tasks can be accomplished in many ways. The following suggestions from Mason (1980) and Putnam (1982) describe how to relate writing to drawing and painting, making functional use of print, and encouraging children to try to read or tell stories they have heard.

Drawing and painting can be tied to writing by encouraging children to print their names on all pictures they make and later by asking children to label their pictures or to construct stories that tell about the pictures. Children can use an invented spelling approach to describe their ideas or watch as the teacher prints out the information that children dictate below the picture. Eventually, they can take over the printing task.

Children can easily learn to recognize their names. Children's names can be used for roll call and written on cards for them to play with or refer to when labeling pictures. Sign and label reading can be extended with walks around the school and neighborhood to identify and copy signs. Children can collect favorite words from home, and words children want to know can be written on cards for them to collect.

Favorite stories that are listened to again and again are often memorized, and children imagine they are reading. A listening post allows children to choose and hear taped stories. The teacher should allow children to pick out their favorite books for the teacher to reread.

Stress a Multifaceted Approach to Literacy

Learning to read using a problem-solving approach requires the use of diverse materials and a wide variety of tasks that are directly or indirectly related to reading, writing, speaking, and listening. Children begin to realize that reading can be woven into most of their work and play activities when their own language, background experiences, and concepts are related to printed materials. Having children act out stories, use picture books to stimulate oral language, observe reading, and develop their writing are examples of this principle.

Paley (1981), who taped and transcribed children's activities, often had children discuss and act out the stories that she read to them. Many of the discussions continued over several days as children asked questions, experimented with solutions, and discussed their interpretations. The children actively searched for meaningful answers and explanations to stories.

Gambrell and Sokolski (1983) recommended the use of picture storybooks to stimulate children's oral language development. They recommended Caldecott Award–winning books because their illustrations have a high "picture/language potency." They suggested showing children the illustrations in a book and asking them what they think will happen, modeling how to study storybook pictures by explaining how a picture helps the reader understand the story, encouraging children to look at the pictures as they tell the story to themselves, having children take turns telling the story while they look at the pictures or work in pairs to tell a story to each other, and arranging times for children to dramatize or tape-record their version of a story.

McCormick and Mason (1984) recommended that adults sometimes talk about parts of the book, saying, for example, "Here's the name [or title] of the book" (pointing to the title), "Here's the beginning of the story," "Here's the first word," "This is the way we read" (running a finger from left to right under a line of print), "Now we read the next page" (turning the page or letting the child know that the left page has been read), and "This is the end."

Rereading favorite stories can help children learn the procedures for reading books and give them an appreciation for story reading. McCormick and Mason (1984) found that an effective approach is for adults to show the cover of a book, name the title, and ask children to say what the book might be about. After reading and discussing a story they can encourage the children to help read it and later have the children read it without an adult's help. Rereading is fostered by keeping the books where the children can easily reach them, by suggesting that children read to one another, and by making photocopies available for them to take home.

Milz (1985) pointed out that writing can be developed before children begin reading. For example, ownership and identity can be established by labeling possessions, papers, pictures, and books; markers can identify coathooks and desks; and books can be signed out by the children. Written communication can be built by using mailboxes for each child and the teacher; personal notes can be sent to individuals and from the teacher. Children often use pictures as well as print to explain what is happening. Some will begin to record special events and, as they become acquainted with good stories and authors, create their own stories.

Foster Active Processing by the Child

Learning to read is an active process when the child uses a problem-solving approach to read and write. Adults should help children relate familiar information (letters, words, stories) to new information and interpreted in terms of their existing knowledge. When the new information does not fit, they should be helped to find a new way to organize the information. This approach requires instruction that is centered on the child's ever-changing, improving constructs and interpretations about how to read, write, take part in classroom discussions, and listen. Reading and writing activities can include listening to stories, and reading and writing attempts.

Although listening to stories is an important and popular kindergarten activity, a more complete support for literacy entails discussion of the story. Children need to express the important story ideas, interpret the characters' actions, make predictions about what might happen, and analyze story motives and outcomes. The teacher can go back over the story after it has been read with a discussion or have children act out the important events.

Discussion can follow the story reading, or children can be coached to retell a story (Morrow, 1984). The structural elements of a story can be featured by reminding children to begin their story with "Once upon a time," encouraging them to introduce the characters and describe the story setting. They may then be asked to tell what the main character wanted to do, what happened, and how it ended.

Discussion of the story can help to foster not only concepts about how stories are structured but also children's listening comprehension and oral language abilities. The story information can excite children about reading as well as help to increase their vocabulary and knowledge of concepts. Finally, hearing written language helps children see how authors convey ideas in stories, how stories are organized, and how written language is different from, or the same as, their own oral language.

Learning to write can occur before children read. To encourage writing, Graves (1981) sets up conferences in which children are asked about the ideas that they have written or pictured. After a conference they can go back and expand, revise, and correct their ideas. Control of the writing process and the topic is in this way left in the hands of the child writer.

When children begin to write, teachers can help children set up and keep word banks (lists of common words needed in their writing), and they can establish a writing environment by setting up written conversations with them and responding in writing to their drafts and questions. Children should keep in writing folders a collection of everything they have written. Then, when a piece is finished, children may show their best work. One way is "Author's Chair Time," in which children meet as a group and a child author sits in the chair, reads the story to the class, and helps lead a discussion about it afterward. Another way is "Publication," in which children rewrite the piece carefully, illustrate and tape or staple it together, put on a hard cover, and place it in the library corner for everyone to read.

SUMMARY

Until recently, kindergartens were designed to foster a positive attitude toward school and provide a well-rounded development through the use of suitable play, art, and social activities. As kindergarten programs have become almost universal, they are critically scrutinized. With newer perspectives about how young children learn and what they ought to be taught about how to read, with more than half the children having already attended preschool or day care programs, and with school administrators and parents having expressed concern that early reading instruction is inadequate, kindergarten reading programs are undergoing change.

Unfortunately, many kindergarten programs have begun to rely on inappropriate materials and techniques taken from formal first-grade programs. The argument is made here that a problem-solving approach is a better model for kindergarten reading and that it can be applied in the context of kindergarten activities. A kindergarten child (Mason, Stewart, & Dunning, 1986) describes this view through her explanation of how she is learning to read at home and at school:

At home I read books and play school with my sister. She's two.
I be the teacher. I read. I'm a good reader by sounding out words.
[At school] she lets us read in class the books. She lets us read sentences.
We put the writing [dictated stories] and we read them to ourselves.
She lets us sound out words. She tells us to sound it out. She tells us
to look at the picture and that tells us what they are doing and then
you can read it (p. 110).

REFERENCES

Bloom, B. (1956). *Taxonomy of educational objectives.* New York: David McKay.
Bloom, B. (1976). *Human characteristics and school learning.* New York: Mc-
Graw-Hill.
Bruner, J., Goodnow, J., & Austin, G. (1956). *A study of thinking.* New York:
Wiley.
Canney, G., & Winograd, P. (1979). *Schemata for reading and reading com-
prehension performance* (Tech. Rep. no. 120). Urbana: University of Illinois,
Center for the Study of Reading.
DiVesta, F., Hayward, K., & Orlando, V. (1979). Developmental trends in
monitoring text for comprehension. *Child Development, 50,* 97–105.
Dunning, D., & Mason, J. (1984). An investigation of kindergarten children's
expressions of story characters' intentions. Paper presented at the National
Reading Conference, St. Petersburg, FL.
Durkin, D. (1968). When should children begin to read? In H. Robinson (Ed.),
Innovation and change in reading instruction, (pp. 30–71). Sixty-seventh
Yearbook of the National Society for the Study of Education, Pt. 2. Chicago:
University of Chicago Press.
Elsasser, N., & John-Steiner, V. (1977). An interactionist approach to advanc-
ing literacy. *Harvard Educational Review, 47,* 355–369.
Fischer, P., & Mandl, H. (1982). Metacognitive regulation of text-processing:
Aspects and problems concerning the relation between self-statements and
actual performance. Paper presented at the American Educational Research
Association Convention, New York.
Flavell, J. (1981). Cognitive monitoring. In W. Dickson (Ed.), *Children's oral
communication skills* (pp. 35–60). New York: Academic Press.
Gambrell, L., & Sokolski, C. (1983). Picture potency: Use Caldecott Award books
to develop children's language. *Reading Teacher, 36,* 868–871.
Garner, R. (1980). Monitoring of understanding: An investigation of good and
poor readers' awareness of induced miscomprehension of text. *Journal of
Reading Behavior, 12,* 55–64.
Garner, R. (1981). Monitoring or passage consistency among poor comprehenders:
A preliminary test of the "piecemeal processing" explanation. *Journal of
Educational Research, 74,* 159–164.

Garner, R., & Alexander, P. (1982). Strategic processing of text: An investigation of the effect on adults' question-answering performance. *Journal of Educational Research, 75,* 144–148.

Gates, A., & Bond, G. (1936). Reading readiness: A study of factors determining success and failure in beginning reading. *Teachers College Record, 37,* 679–685.

Graves, D. (1981). Patterns of child control of the writing process. In R. Walshe (Ed.). *Donald Graves in Australia* (pp. 17–28). Rosebery, NSW: Primary English Teaching Association.

Hare, V. (1981). Readers' problem identification and problem-solving strategies for high- and low-knowledge comprehenders. *Journal of Reading Behavior, 13,* 159–165.

Hare, V., & Pulliam, C. (1980). College students' metacognitive awareness of reading behavior. In M. Kamil & A. Moe (Eds.), *Perspectives on reading research and instruction* (pp. 226–231). Rochester, NY: National Reading Conference.

Heath, S. (1983). *Ways with words: Language, life and work in communities and classrooms.* Cambridge: Cambridge University Press.

Hunt, J. (1983). *The role of early experience in the development of intelligence and personality.* Champaign: University of Illinois.

Inhelder, B., & Piaget, J. (1958). *The growth of logical thinking from childhood to adolescence.* New York: Basic Books.

James, W. (1890). *Principles of psychology: Vol. 1.* New York: Holt.

Markman, E. (1979). Realizing that you don't understand: Elementary school children's awareness of inconsistencies. *Child Development, 50,* 643–655.

Markman, E. (1981). Comprehension monitoring. In W. Dickson (Ed.), *Children's oral communication skills* (pp. 61–84). New York: Academic Press.

Mason, J. (1976). Overgeneralization in learning to read. *Journal of Reading Behavior, 8,* 173–181.

Mason, J. (1980). When *do* children begin to read: An exploration of four-year-old children's letter and word reading competencies. *Reading Research Quarterly, 15,* 203–226.

Mason, J. (1985). Cognitive monitoring and early reading: A proposed model. In D. Forrest, G. MacKinnon, & T. Waller (Eds.), *Meta-cognition, cognition, and human performance* (pp. 77–102). New York: Academic Press.

Mason, J., & Au, K. (1984). Learning social context characteristics in prereading lessons. In J. Flood (Ed.), *Promoting reading comprehension.* Newark, DE: International Reading Association.

Mason, J., & Au, K. (1986). *Reading instruction for today.* Glenview, IL: Scott Foresman.

Mason, J., McCormick, C., & Bhavnagri, N. (1983). How are you going to help me learn? Lesson negotiations between a teacher and preschool children. Paper presentation at the Society for Research in Child Development convention, Detroit.

Mason, J., Stewart, J., & Dunning, D. (1986). Measuring early reading: A window into kindergarten children's understanding. In T. Raphael with R.

Reynolds (Eds.), *Contexts of school-based literacy* (pp. 97–113). New York: Random House.

McCormick, C., & Mason, J. (1984). *Intervention procedures for increasing preschool children's interest in and knowledge about reading* (Tech. Rep. no. 312). Urbana: University of Illinois, Center for the Study of Reading.

McGraw, M. (1935). *Growth: A study of Johnny and Jimmy.* New York: Appleton-Century.

Menyuk, P. (1984). Language development and reading. In J. Flood (Ed.), *Understanding reading comprehension* (pp. 101–121). Newark, DE: International Reading Association.

Meyers, M., & Paris, S. (1978). Children's metacognitive knowledge about reading. *Journal of Educational Psychology, 70,* 680–690.

Milz, V. (1985). First graders' uses for writing. In A. Jaggar & M. Smith-Burke (Eds.), *Observing the language learner* (pp. 173–189). Newark, NJ: International Reading Association.

Morphett, V. & Washburne, C. (1931). When should children begin to read? *Elementary School Journal, 31,* 495–503.

Morrow, L. (1984). Effects of story retelling on young children's comprehension and sense of story structure. In J. Niles & L. Harris (Eds.), *Changing perspectives on research in reading/language processing and instruction* (pp. 95–100). Rochester, NY: National Reading Conference.

Olson, D. (1984). "See! Jumping!" Some oral language antecedents of literacy. In H. Goelman, A. Oberg, & F. Smith (Eds.), *Awakening to literacy* (pp. 185–192). Exeter, NH: Heinemann.

Owings, R., Peterson, G., Bransford, J., Morris, C., & Stein, B. (1980). Spontaneous monitoring and regulation of learning: A comparison of successful and less successful fifth graders. *Journal of Educational Psychology, 72,* 250–256.

Paley, V. (1981). *Wally's stories.* Cambridge: Harvard University Press.

Paris, S., & Meyers, M. (1981). Comprehension monitoring memory and study strategies of good and poor readers. *Journal of Reading Behavior, 13,* 5–22.

Peterman, C., Dunning, D., & Mason, J. (1985). *A storybook reading event: How a teacher's presentation affects kindergarten children's subsequent attempts to read from the text.* Paper presentation at the National Reading Conference, San Diego, CA.

Putnam, L. (1982). *A descriptive study of two philosophically different approaches to reading readiness, as they were used in six inner city kindergartens.* ERIC document no. ED 220, 807, CS 006 795.

Reeve, R., & Brown, A. (1984). *Metacognition reconsidered: Implications for intervention research* (Tech. Rep. no. 328). Urbana, IL: University of Illinois, Center for the Study of Reading.

Resnick, D., & Resnick, L. (1977). The nature of literacy: An historical exploration. *Harvard Educational Review, 47,* 370–385.

Robinson, E., & Robinson, W. (1976). Developmental changes in the child's understanding of communication failure. *Australian Journal of Psychology, 28,* 155–165

Schieffelin, B., & Cochran-Smith, M. (1984). Learning to read culturally: Literacy before schooling. In H. Goelman, A. Oberg, & F. Smith (Eds.), *Awakening to literacy* (pp. 3–23). Exeter, NH: Heinemann.

Siegler, R. (1978). The origins of scientific reasoning. In R. Siegler (Ed.), *Children's thinking: What develops?* New York: Wiley.

Skinner, B. F. (1953). *Science and human behavior* (pp. 109–149). New York: Holt, Rinehart and Winston.

Smith, N. B. (1965). *American reading instruction*. Newark, DE: International Reading Association.

Snow, C., & Ninio, A. (1986). The contracts of literacy: What children learn from learning to read books. In W. Teale & E. Sulzby (Eds.), *Emergent literacy: Writing and reading*. Norwood, NJ: Ablex.

Teale, W., & Sulzby, E. (1986). Emergent literacy as a perspective for examining how young children become writers and readers. In W. Teale & E. Sulzby (Eds.), *Emergent literacy: Writing and reading*. Norwood, NJ: Ablex.

Thomas, L. (1980). The relationship between good and poor readers' awareness of reading schemata and their performance on a measure of reading comprehension. Ph.D. diss., University of Maryland.

Wagoner, S. (1983). Comprehension monitoring: What it is and what we know about it. *Reading Research Quarterly, 18*, 328–346.

Wells, G. (1981). *Learning through interaction: The study of language development*. Cambridge: Cambridge University Press.

CHAPTER 5

Cognitive Learning and Development

Constance Kamii

Cognition refers to the "act or process of knowing." As the title of this chapter suggests, there is a difference between children's learning and their development of knowledge. *Cognitive learning* refers to the acquisition of specific information, while *cognitive development* denotes knowledge of a more general nature. For example, "Washington is the capital of the United States" is a specific bit of knowledge, but this statement cannot be understood without a general framework that enables a person to know what a capital and the United States are. This framework takes many years to develop and cannot be taught directly to children. It can be built only by each child, through his own mental action.

Many educators and psychologists do not distinguish between learning and development. They believe that all knowledge must be acquired by the child through internalization of information from the environment and that an individual's knowledge is the sum total of all the specific bits that have been taught. Others are convinced that there is a more general, internal process called development and that teaching everything is both unnecessary and impossible. Kindergarten is where these views clash more directly than at any other grade level.

The source and nature of human knowledge have been the subject of long debates among epistemologists since the time of the Greeks. Epistemology is a branch of philosophy concerned with the origin, nature, and limits of human knowing. Epistemologists study questions such as "How do we know what we think we know?" and "How do we know that what we think we know is true?"

Two currents of thought have developed through the centuries in response to these questions: the empiricist and rationalist currents. Empiricists such as Locke (1632–1704), Berkeley (1685–1753), and Hume (1711–1776) argued in essence that knowledge has its source outside the individual and that it is internalized through the senses. They further argued that the individual at birth is like a clean slate on which experiences are "written" as the person grows up. As Locke stated in 1690, "The senses at first let in particular ideas, and furnish the yet empty cabinet, and the mind by degrees growing familiar with some of them, they are lodged in the memory" (1947, p. 22).

Rationalists such as Descartes (1596–1650), Spinoza (1632–1677), and Kant (1724–1804) did not deny the importance of sensory experience, but they insisted that reason is more powerful than sensory experience because it enables us to know with certainty many truths that sensory observation can never ascertain. For example, we know that every event has a cause, in spite of the fact that we cannot examine every event in the entire past and future of the universe. Rationalists also pointed out that since our senses often deceive us (e.g., perceptual illusions), sensory experience cannot be trusted to give us reliable knowledge. The rigor, precision, and certainty of mathematics, a purely deductive discipline, remains the rationalists' prime example in support of the power of reason. When they had to explain the origin of this power, rationalists ended up by saying that certain concepts are innate and that they unfold as a function of maturation.

Piaget saw elements of truth and untruth in both camps. As a 20th century scientist with a Doctor of Natural Sciences degree in biology, he was convinced that the only way to answer epistemological questions was to study them scientifically rather than by speculation. With this conviction, he decided that a good way to study the relationship between empirical knowledge and reason in humans was to study their development in children. The 60 years he spent studying children's cognitive development were thus a means to answer epistemological questions scientifically.

Until the early part of the 20th century, education was based entirely on common sense, opinions, and tradition, without any scientific knowledge about how human beings learn. The scientific study of learning and development is a relatively recent phenomenon both in psychology and in education. The result is that while other professions such as medicine, engineering, architecture, and agriculture have come to base their practices on scientific knowledge, education is still at a prescientific stage.[1] When asked how children learn number concepts, for example, teachers give the most naive, commonsensical, vague, and contradictory explanations such as "from sets of objects," "by learning to count,"

---

[1]Some people may say (a) that it is not enough for education to have scientific knowledge and (b) that scientific research exists in education. I agree that education is an art, and that it is not enough to have scientific knowledge. However, education must become an art based on scientific knowledge just as medicine has advanced to the stage of becoming an art based on scientific knowledge. I also agree that scientific research exists in education. However, this research has focused on very limited aspects of knowledge rather than

"through one-to-one correspondence," "by manipulating objects," and "from experience." Physicians know when they do not know the cause of certain diseases such as cancer. Many educators, by contrast, are not even aware that they do not know how children acquire number concepts and try only to get children to produce correct answers.

The 20th century has seen a considerable amount of research on human learning and children's cognitive development. However, none of the researchers except Piaget has studied the nature and development of human knowledge as an organized whole. The studies of learning theorists such as E. Thorndike, Skinner, Hull, Gagné, Wertheimer, Lewin, Osgood, Newell, Shaw, Simon, Hebb, Miller, Galanter, and Pribram are too circumscribed to be useful to educators. Since educators must conceptualize educational goals and objectives, they need to understand how children acquire knowledge as a whole. The studies of developmental psychologists such as Gesell, Werner, J. Baldwin, and Hall are broader and closer to children's real life but are too heterogeneous (Gesell), normative, static, or limited to guide educators in conceptualizing objectives. Many developmental psychologists have studied children's development in specific areas such as space, number, and classification, but these fragmentary findings do not enable us to conceptualize a total kindergarten curriculum aimed at stimulating children's cognitive development. Objectives for kindergarten education have been defined by tradition and opinions such as those of Froebel, Montessori, Harriet Johnson, Dewey, and many others who shared the child-development view in Boston, Detroit, Iowa, Minnesota, and New York, and by the pendulum that swings between new fads and regression. The pendulum now is at the extreme called "back to basics," the demand of a society threatened by foreign competition.

Piaget's theory seems more useful for curriculum development than any other scientific theory of learning or development because the questions he studied were the broadest and most precise ones about all aspects of human knowledge. Some of the questions he studied were: How do we know what we think we know? What is logic? What is its origin? What is science? How did it evolve from prehistoric time? Why and how does it continue to develop? How is new knowledge created in scientific revolutions? What is mathematics? Did it develop the same way as physics or differently? What are time and space? What are the biological mechanisms of development? His focus was thus not only the individual's life

---

on knowledge as it develops as an organized whole from infancy to adulthood. It has also focused on peripheral issues such as changes in behavior and the effects of "homogeneous" grouping.

span but also biology and the history of knowledge of the entire human race.[2] As will be shown later, his theory called constructivism is a synthesis of empiricism and rationalism that goes beyond both of these earlier views.

In this chapter, I will discuss what we know about how children construct knowledge. I will focus mainly on children of kindergarten age, but younger and older children's knowledge will also be mentioned, since the cognitive development of kindergarten children can be understood only by knowing what comes before and after this age. The chapter will conclude with a brief discussion of the implications of Piaget's theory for conceptualizing goals and objectives. As Kohlberg and Mayer (1972) have said, the most important issues confronting educators is the choice of ends for the educative process. Without valid goals, it is impossible to decide which educational programs achieve objectives of importance and which teach facts and skills that do not contribute to children's further development.

HOW CHILDREN ACQUIRE KNOWLEDGE

The two most important answers I give to the question of children's acquisition of knowledge are (1) that they acquire it by constructing it from the inside in interaction with the environment, and (2) that they construct it as an organized whole. Each of these statements is clarified below.

Educators generally hold the empiricist assumption that children acquire knowledge through a process of internalization of information from the environment. Empiricists, it will be recalled, believe that knowledge has its source outside the individual and is internalized through the senses and language. Piaget showed over and over that this belief is false and that children acquire knowledge by constructing it from the inside out, in interaction with the environment.

A particularly instructive example of children's construction of knowledge is their creation of the geocentric theory (Piaget, 1927/1966, 1926/1967). In the 1920s the children Piaget interviewed had a variety of theories about how the sun moved (by its own will, God, the wind,

---

[2]Piaget (1932/1965) also studied the nature and development of morality in the individual and in human history. While questions of right and wrong are highly relevant to education, they are beyond the scope of this chapter, which concerns only knowledge, i.e., questions of what is true or untrue.

etc.). Today these ideas are sometimes replaced by rockets and astronauts. Here is how Jamie responded when he was almost five:

> How did the sun get up in the sky? — *A rocket.* . . . — How did the rocket put the sun in the sky? — *It can get up there.* . . . *A person stayed in the rocket.* . . . — Does the sun move? — *Yes.* — How does it move? — (No response) — Is the sun alive? — *No.* . . . — Is it up in the sky all the time? — *Not in the night.* — Where does it go at night? — *It sleeps.* — Does it wake up? — *Yes.* — When does it wake up? — *In the morning.*

Note that Jamie was inconsistent. After saying that the sun is not alive, he stated that it goes to sleep at night and wakes up in the morning. This illogic is a characteristic of young children's thinking until 7 or 8 years of age — the beginning of the stage Piaget characterized as "operational" (which roughly means "logical").[3]

Children do not wait to be instructed to acquire knowledge. They are busy trying to make sense out of everything they encounter. They construct the geocentric theory because they put into relationships the empirical facts that are knowable by them. Adult scientists, too, constructed the geocentric theory and believed it until the 16th century, after Copernicus's publication of the heliocentric theory. What spurred him to go beyond the old empirical knowledge was a desire to eliminate the incoherence caused by the corrections, and corrections of corrections, that were necessary in the old way of thinking.

Educators generally define objectives according to traditional disciplines and, within each discipline, often teach one unrelated "concept" after another (such as "more than," "circles and squares," and pennies, nickels, and dimes in a typical kindergarten math program). Piaget's research (1937/1954, 1967/1971, 1975), however, showed that each child constructs his or her knowledge as an organized whole.

He distinguished three kinds of knowledge according to their ultimate sources and modes of structuring: physical knowledge, logico-mathematical knowledge, and social (conventional) knowledge (Piaget, 1932/

---

[3]Operations are (mental) actions that have become reversible and been combined (grouped) with others of the same system. Class inclusion and the measurement of length and time are examples of concrete operations that will be discussed shortly.

The stage before the appearance of concrete operations around 7 or 8 years of age is called "preoperational." No one before Piaget knew that young children reasoned in such preposterously nonsensical ways. Many educators today are still unaware that young children think so differently from adults.

1965, 1950a, 1950b, 1950c, 1967/1971, 1970). I will clarify each first and later discuss how in reality knowledge develops as an inseparable whole.

Physical, Logico-Mathematical, and Social (Conventional) Knowledge

Physical knowledge is knowledge of objects in external reality. The color and weight of a pencil are examples of physical properties that are *in* objects in external reality, and can be known by observation. The knowledge that a pencil breaks when we press too hard on it is also an example of physical knowledge.

Logico-mathematical knowledge, on the other hand, consists of relationships created by each individual. For instance, when we are presented with a red pencil and a black one and think that they are different, this difference is an example of logico-mathematical knowledge. The pencils are indeed observable, but the difference between them is not. The difference is neither *in* the red pencil nor *in* the black one, and if a person did not put the objects into this relationship, the difference would not exist for him. Other examples of relationships an individual can create between the pencils are "similar," "the same in weight," and "two." It is just as correct to say that the red and black pencils are similar as it is to say that they are different, because relationships do not exist "out there" in external, observable reality.

Social (conventional) knowledge is knowledge that has its source in conventions created by people. Examples of social knowledge are the fact that Christmas comes on December 25, that pencils are called "pencils," and that tables are not to stand on. The main characteristic of social knowledge is that is is largely arbitrary in nature. The fact that some people celebrate Christmas while others do not is an example of the arbitrariness of social knowledge. There is no physical or logical reason for December 25 to be any different from any other day of the year. The fact that a pencil is called "pencil" is likewise completely arbitrary. In another language, the same object is called by another name. It follows that, for the child to acquire social knowledge, input from people is necessary.

Having made a theoretical distinction among three kinds of knowledge, Piaget went on to say that in the psychological reality of the child, the three develop together inseparably, especially during infancy and early childhood (Piaget, 1937/1954, 1967/1971). For example, the child could not construct the relationship "different" (logico-mathematical knowledge) if all the objects in the world had identical properties (physical knowledge). Similarly, the relationship "two" would be impossible to make if the child thought that discrete objects behaved like drops of water that combine to become one drop.

While logico-mathematical knowledge thus depends on physical knowledge for its construction, the converse is also true, because the child needs a logico-mathematical framework to "read" empirical facts from reality. For example, to note that a pencil is red, the child needs a classificatory scheme to distinguish "red" from all other colors. He also needs a classificatory scheme to distinguish "pencils" from all the other kinds of objects he already knows. A logico-mathematical framework is thus necessary for the construction of physical knowledge because a child could not "read" any fact from external reality if each fact were an isolated bit of knowledge with no relationship to the knowledge already built and organized by him or her.

Social knowledge is like physical knowledge in that it is knowledge of content that requires a logico-mathematical framework for its construction. Just as the child needs a logico-mathematical framework to recognize a red pencil mark as such, he or she needs the same framework to recognize it as "the teacher's" in opposition to his or her own writing with a black pencil. The following example illustrates the need for a logico-mathematical framework for the child to get social knowledge from reality. A child who saw his grandfather praying before a meal for the first time asked his mother, "Why does Grandpa read his plate?" Children construct their logico-mathematical framework as they construct their knowledge of contents.

Logico-Mathematical Knowledge

In the preceding discussion I referred to logico-mathematical *knowledge* as well as to the logico-mathematical *framework*. The latter is part of the former (Piaget, 1967/1971). Part of logico-mathematical knowledge is a framework that serves to organize contents like physical and social knowledge, and part of it consists of logic and mathematics, which are contentless and begin to appear around 7 or 8 years of age.

Mathematics includes both arithmetic and geometry, and Piaget further differentiated the logico-mathematical framework into the logico-arithmetical and the spatio-temporal frameworks (Piaget, 1946/1969, 1967/1971). All events are understood through these frameworks, and our knowledge of astronomy, mechanics, history, and so on, is all organized with them. To understand who Abraham Lincoln was, for example, we must put him in a category (President) in a place (the United States) and a time (1861–1865). As children increase their knowledge of contents, they construct these frameworks by extending them and organizing them hierarchically with increasing coherence.

We were raised to believe that time and space were empirical knowledge that could simply be "discovered." Piaget, however, showed that these are systems of relationships that have to be constructed by each child. Below is an example from *The Child's Conception of Time* (Piaget, 1946/1969). Piaget asked children between 4 and 9 years of age about age differences. MYR, a 5-year-old who had a sister, responded in the following way:

> Is she older or younger than you? — *Older.* — And when you grow up to be a lady, will she still be older than you? — *I don't know. She'll be a lady.* — Can one tell if your sister will always remain older than you? — *Yes, one can tell, but I can't myself.* (p. 223)

Time is a framework, or a system of temporal relationships, that children construct for themselves over many years. Young children have not constructed it and therefore cannot deduce that the interval between their own birth and a sibling's birth will always remain the same. Young children therefore use the best means they have to get information — the empirical knowledge of size and statements made by other people.

Similar observations can be made in classrooms. One day in a kindergarten room, three children were discussing their birthdays, which were coming up that month according to the list of special events for the month posted on the wall. The children were saying that Jake's birthday was to come first and then Andrea's and then Dee-Dee's. "Who is the oldest?" the teacher asked them, and they answered in unison, "Andrea." She went on to inquire how they knew that, and the children explained, "Because she is the biggest." The teacher knew that it would be useless to correct the children.

Space, too, is a framework, or a system of spatial relationships, that each child has to construct. The simplest example can be seen in young children's drawings of trees on mountains. Their trees are perpendicular to the side of the mountain and not to a horizontal line of a larger frame of reference. Their chimneys are likewise perpendicular to the roofs they draw (Piaget & Inhelder, 1948/1967).

A more sophisticated example from Piaget's (1951/1976) research is the following. He asked children between 5 and 15 years of age what Switzerland was and what Geneva was and went on to ask them to draw Switzerland in relation to a circle he drew to show Geneva. Before 7 or 8 years of age, the children typically responded in the following way:

Claude (6 years 9 months of age): What is Switzerland? — *It's a country.* — And Geneva? — *A town.* — Where is Geneva? — *In Switzerland.* (The child draws the two circles side by side but the circle for Geneva is smaller.) *I'm drawing the circle for Geneva smaller because Geneva is smaller. Switzerland is very big.* — Quite right, but where is Geneva? — *In Switzerland.* — Are you Swiss? — *Yes.* — And are you Genevese? — *Oh, no! I'm Swiss now.* (p. 40)

While young children may use language correctly, their spatial relationships may be different from ours. This example is complicated by the fact that countries and towns are social knowledge and not observable. However, they are also categories and spatial extensions that have to be organized hierarchically.

I would like to make an important point about children's wrong answers. While educators generally do not have any respect for them, Piaget believed that children made errors *because* they are intelligent and that in every error are elements of correctness. For example, Claude was careful to make Switzerland bigger than Geneva. When he said that one could not be both Swiss and Genevese at the same time, this idea was consistent with the spatial relationship he made between Switzerland and Geneva. Knowledge thus develops in a messy and complicated way, and the development of one part depends on the development of other parts.

Following is a similar example from the United States. One day, as I was walking in a hallway, I came face to face with a kindergarten girl sitting on the floor. When she saw me, she greeted me with "Hi, Chinese," as black children often do. I told her that I was Japanese, not Chinese, and decided to ask, "What are *you*?" She answered, "I'm black," and I went on with "And are you American?" To my surprise, she replied that she was, and I told her that I, too, was an American. She was very puzzled, and the next question she asked was "Is that because you are black?" Nationality belongs to social knowledge, while racial characteristics belong to physical knowledge. (The physical knowledge, however, is complicated by the fact that the color of black children's skin is not really black.) For this child, *American* seemed to be almost another word for *black*, but she was not sure whether all Americans were black.

Starting around seven or eight years of age, children develop logic and number out of the logico-arithmetical framework, and spatial and temporal operations out of the spatio-temporal framework. Each of these domains will now be discussed.

Logic. Young children's reactions to the class-inclusion task illustrate well how they begin to construct logic (Inhelder & Piaget, 1959/1964).

In this task, the child is presented with six miniature dogs and two cats of the same size, for example, and is first asked, "What do you see?" so that the examiner can proceed with whatever word came from the child's vocabulary. The child is then asked to show "*all* the animals," "*all* the dogs," and "*all* the cats" with the words that came from his vocabulary (e.g., "doggies"). Only after ascertaining the child's understanding of the words involved does the adult ask the following class-inclusion question: "Are there more dogs or more animals?"

Four-year-olds typically answer, "More dogs," whereupon the adult asks, "Than what?" Four-year-olds usually reply, "Than cats." In other words, the question the examiner asks is "Are there more dogs or more animals?" but the question young children "hear" is "Are there more dogs or more cats?" Young children hear a question that is different from the one the adult asked because once they have mentally cut the whole into two parts, the only thing they can think about is the two parts. For them, at that moment, the whole no longer exists. They can think about the whole and the parts *successively* in time, but not *simultaneously*. In order to compare the whole with a part, the child has to do two opposite mental actions at the same time: cut the whole into two parts and put the parts back together into a whole. This is precisely what 4-year-olds cannot do.

By 7 or 8 years of age, most children's thought becomes mobile enough to be reversible. Reversibility is the ability to mentally do opposite actions simultaneously — in this case, to separate the whole into two parts and reunite the parts into a whole. In physical, material action, it is not possible to do two opposite things simultaneously. In our heads, however, this is possible, when thought has become mobile enough to be reversible. It is only when the parts can be reunited in the mind that a child can "see" that there are more animals than dogs.

The quantification of classes and subclasses is attained earlier or later depending on contents. If we ask children whether there are more boys or more children (or more girls or more children), this question is answered more easily than the one concerning dogs and animals. If we present them with pictures of ducks, other birds, and other animals such as a horse, a fish, a mouse, and a snake, and ask them "Are there more ducks or more birds?" this question is harder than the one about more dogs or more animals. Some contents are thus harder to structure logically, partly because they are less familiar and partly because their physical properties are more ambiguous.[4]

---

[4]This explanation, which differs from the one given by Inhelder and Piaget (1959/1964, p. 117), is mine.

Class inclusion is later used in adolescence, when formal operations become possible. Formal operations are operations on concrete operations, such as class inclusion. Examples of formal operations can be found in our ability to perform scientific experiments by considering all the possible hypotheses and testing them systematically one by one. Following is an often-mentioned example about the flexibility of metal rods (Inhelder & Piaget, 1955/1958).

The child is given a number of metal rods, weights of 100, 200, and 300 grams, and an apparatus that can hold seven rods apart horizontally. He or she is shown how to adjust the screws to change the rods as well as the length of each rod. The child is also shown how each weight can be screwed onto the end of each rod to make it (the rod) bend. In addition, his or her attention is called to the fact that some of the rods are made of brass and some of steel, that some are round and some are square, and that some are fat while others are skinny. After thus being shown all the different factors that can make a rod bend a lot or a little bit, the child is asked (1) to find out experimentally the factors that affect the flexibility of the rods and (2) to prove his or her conclusion.

In the period of concrete operations, the child can easily classify the rods by any of their properties and name all of them. However, in experimenting with the objects, 9-year-olds typically compare any rod with any other rod, thinking only of two or three properties at a time. Thus, they may pick up a long, thin, round, steel rod, and compare it with one that is short, thick, round and made of steel. Asked if this comparison was better than one involving two short rods differing only in width, a 9-year-old even replied that it was better because it made the rods "more different" (p. 50)! The child who holds all other factors constant and systematically compares only one difference at a time can be said to have formal operations.

The shocking revelation of recent research is that the attainment of formal operations is rare even among college freshmen. These students were successful enough in elementary and secondary schools to get into universities. Yet the percentage of freshmen found to be capable of solid formal operations was 25 % at the University of Oklahoma (McKinnon & Renner, 1971) and 20 % at Rutgers University (Schwebel, 1975). These low percentages can be explained by the fact that schools generally emphasize "right" answers and seldom encourage children to think critically.

I stated earlier that the source of logico-mathematical knowledge is in each child because relationships do not exist "out there" in external reality. The ability to include a class in a higher-order class originates in each child, who puts objects into relationships of "the same" and "different." By coordinating the relationships he thus made among "dogs," "cats," and "animals" or among "rods made of brass," "those made of steel," "long ones," "short ones," "fat ones," "skinny ones," "square ones," "round ones," "those with a heavy weight on them," and "those with a light weight," the child becomes able to think logically. One of the major contributions of Piaget's theory is that it thus showed that the source of children's ability to think logically is *in* each child, not *in* the teacher.

Number. The limitation of empirical knowledge can again be seen in the child's construction of number. The task that shows this construction well uses two identical glasses (one for the child and one for the experimenter) and 50 to 70 beads or chips (Inhelder & Piaget, 1963). The child is asked to drop one bead into his glass each time the experimenter drops one in hers, sometimes saying "bing . . . bing . . . bing . . . " to ensure the simultaneity of the one-to-one correspondence. After seven or eight beads are thus dropped, the experimenter says, "Let's stop now, and *you* watch what I am going to do." In front of the child's watchful eyes, she drops one bead into her glass and proceeds to say to the child, "Let's get going again." When both have dropped about 7 more beads and the following situation exists, the experimenter asks, "Do we both have the same amount, or do *you* have more, or do *I* have more?"

Experimenter: $1+1+1+1+1+1+1+1+1+1+1+1+1+1+1$

Child: $1+1+1+1+1+1+1$ $+1+1+1+1+1+1+1+1$

Four-year- olds typically reply, "I have more," or "We have the same amount." When we ask them how they know that they have more, they typically say nothing more than "Because." On the other hand, when we ask them how they know that the two glasses contain the same amount, they explain "Because I can see that they have the same amount." The examiner then asks the child how the beads were dropped, and 4-year-olds usually report every empirical fact correctly ("We dropped them at the same time, and we stopped for a while, and only *you* put one in, and we got going again. . . . "). In other words, these children have all the empirical information they need to give the correct answer but cannot deduce that the experimenter has one more.

By age 5, by contrast, most children say that the experimenter has one more and invoke the same empirical facts to justify their conclusion. Number thus grows out of children's ability to think logically. If they can make logical relationships among the beads, they make the correct numerical judgment. If they cannot, the best thing they have to make a quantitative judgment is their eyes, which provide only empirical knowledge.

If a 5-year-old thinks the experimenter has one more bead, we can go on to ask, "What will happen if we keep dropping more beads all night? Do you think we will both have the same amount, or do you think one of us will have more?" Some reply, "You will still have one more," but others say, "We don't have enough beads to do that," or "We can't know because we haven't done it yet." Our adult logic is solid enough to deduce that the difference of 1 will always remain the same, but 5-year-olds' logic is usually not structured that well. (Even adults have trouble thinking about the billions in the federal budget, and all I understand is that it is "a lot" of money!)

The source of number concepts is in each child; therefore number concepts are not teachable. This may seem like bad news for teachers, but the good news is that we do not have to teach numbers because children will construct them by themselves with their own ability to think. Ability to count belongs to social knowledge, and each language has a different set of words to be learned. The underlying numerical ideas, however, belong to logico-mathematical knowledge, which is universal.

Space. Children's construction of ability to measure length is selected (Piaget, Inhelder, & Szeminska, 1948/1964) as an example of a spatial operation because it is included in most primary math programs. *Measurement* refers to the quantification of continuous aspects of reality such as length, time, volume, weight, and temperature. *Number* is different in that it concerns the quantification of collections of objects. Numerical quantification is easier than measurement for two reasons. First, the unit is given in the former, while in the latter it has to be invented and introduced into external reality. Second, measurement is more difficult because it involves an intermediary object that requires transitive thinking.

Transitivity is the ability to make relationships by coordinating smaller relationships. For example, if we know that A > B and that B > C, we can deduce that A is necessarily bigger than C. Young children at the preoperational level cannot make this deduction because they can only make small relationships between two objects at a time. After asking them to compare two sticks at a time, A (10cm) and B (9.7cm), and then B and C (9.4 cm) while hiding A, we can ask them if A is equal to, longer, or shorter than C. Young children reply either by guessing or by saying that they cannot know because they did not see A and C together. Measurement involves an intermediary object such as a stick, and the ability to deduce that if A is as long as the stick, and the stick is longer than B, A is necessarily longer than B.

In chapter 2 of *The Child's Conception of Geometry*, we find a stage (IIIA) when the child has constructed transitivity but not the part–whole relationships necessary for thinking about a unit. Children at this level can compare two towers built apart on tables of different height only if they have a stick that is as long as or longer than the towers. The idea of using a short block over and over as a unit of measurement does not occur to them, and when this possibility is suggested to them, they do not see the utility of the block, or they step it in an approximate way without feeling the need to be exact in this procedure.

Later, around 8 years of age (stage IIIB), children think about using the short block as a unit and count the number of times they step it to measure the height of their towers. Once they have constructed a unit, they can use it in the same way as numbers. Just as children construct numbers with their own natural ability to think, they construct units of length with the same ability. Conventional units such as inches and centimeters belong to social knowledge, but the underlying reasoning is logico-mathematical knowledge, which is universal. Children go on to measure area and volume, too, independently of instruction.

Time. The measurement of time involves the same reasoning as length — transitivity and units. Time is harder, however, because it is not observable at all. Following is an example of a task from *The Child's Conception of Time* (Piaget, 1946/1969).

Piaget showed a sand-glass to the child and let the sand in it run for a certain duration while the child performed a task, such as drawing a horizontal line across a sheet of graph paper by going across one square with each beat of a metronome. The line thus drawn covered 30 squares. After the child drew this line, he was shown a stopwatch and asked to time the movement of the sand in the sand-glass. When the child thus knew that the sand ran while the watch moved "from here to here" (i.e., 30 seconds), he was asked to draw a line again at the same speed as before, using the metronome and stopwatch this time. The question put to him was how long a line would he be able to draw (the same length, a longer one, or a shorter one than before)? Here is a protocol illustrating the thinking of an 8-year-old.

> (PAK, 8;8): Well, how far would the line stretch if we worked with the clock instead of the sand-glass? *One can't tell.* Why? *We must make an experiment first.* But the sand-glass ran up to where? *Up to here.* And aren't the sand-glass and this point (30") on the watch the same thing? *Yes.* So if you worked at the same speed, how far would the clock go? *One can't really tell.* (p. 202)

This child had all the empirical facts we would need to deduce that the line would be as long as before. Yet he could not reason with transitivity and therefore expressed the need to see what would happen. We can see from this example and many others that there is much more to telling time than is assumed by authors of first-grade math books.

The mode of structuring of logico-mathematical knowledge is very different from that of physical and social knowledge. Logico-mathematical knowledge is built by the child by coordinating the relationships he created before. Every later relationship is built with the ones made before, and earlier relationships become integrated into later ones while conserving their earlier forms. Thus, for example, class inclusion remains intact as a part-whole hierarchical organization even when the child goes on to construct formal operations with this earlier structure.

Logico-mathematical structures become more and more independent of content as the child grows older and eventually becomes logic, algebra, and geometry, which are contentless. Physical and social knowledge, by contrast, remains dependent on logico-mathematical knowledge and in fact becomes increasingly more dependent on it. Physics and astronomy are the logico-mathematization of physical knowledge, while economics and political science are the logico-mathematization of social knowledge.

Logico-mathematical knowledge is an intriguing domain that has the following three characteristics with far-reaching implications for education.

First, it is not directly teachable because it is constructed out of relationships the child has created among objects, and every subsequent relationship he or she creates is a relationship based on the relationships created before. This is why a solid foundation is so important for young children to build.

Second, there is only one way in which logico-mathematical knowledge develops, and that is toward more coherence. Because there is nothing arbitrary in logico-mathematical knowledge, if the child constructs it at all, he or she will construct it toward more and more coherence. All normal children will sooner or later have class inclusion without a single lesson in class inclusion.

Third, if logico-mathematical knowledge is constructed once, it will never be forgotten. Once the child believes that there are more animals than dogs, there is no way of convincing him or her that he or she should go back to the earlier way of thinking.

Representation

I have so far been discussing the child's construction of knowledge without clarifying Piaget's theory of representation. It is now necessary to discuss this mental activity. In our empiricist upbringing, we were told that words such as *pencil* represent objects. This is completely erroneous according to Piaget. The representing is done by each person, and words do not represent anything by themselves. Each person gives meaning to words, and this is why the same word often does not mean the same thing to two people. Young children understand words such as *mother, hundred, lies,* and *winning,* but they do not give the same meaning to these words as adults.

Piaget (1946/1962, 1947/1963) distinguished three ways in which we represent objects and ideas: with indices, with symbols, and with signs. An index is part of the object or is causally related to it. For example, the sound we hear from a jet and the trace it leaves behind are indices of a jet. When we hear the sound, we know that there is a jet even if we cannot see it.

In contrast to indices, symbols and signs are not part of the object but exist apart from it. The difference between symbols and signs is that symbols are created by each person and bear a resemblance to the real object. Below are examples of representation with symbols.

1. Thinking about a jet, evoking a mental image of it
2. Pretending
      The child may use his or her body to imitate a jet (zooming around with arms stretched out like the wings of an airplane) or use an object and pretend that it is a jet (e.g., holding two pencils crosswise calling it an "airplane")
3. Recognizing a jet in a picture or a model, or making a picture or model

Signs, such as words, are a part of a system made by convention and do not resemble the object at all. The word *jet,* for instance, does not resemble a jet. Other examples of signs are the Morse code and mathematical signs.

We are often told that representation develops from the pictorial level (sometimes called "semiconcrete" by math educators) to the level of words. However, Piaget's theory states that pictures and words originate from very different sources. Symbols can be invented by each child, but words are made by convention and therefore require input from people. Once the child has constructed the *idea* of four, for example, he can represent it with

"○ ○ ○ ○" or "⚓ ⚓ ⚓ ⚓"

without any instruction. The spoken word *four* and the numeral 4, however, require social transmission.

It follows that all the pictures of sets of objects found in workbooks are useless. They serve to communicate questions when we want to *test* children. However, if *teaching* is our intention, getting children to write "4" next to a picture of four apples is useless. The children who can do this are able to do it because they have already constructed the knowledge of number necessary to do it. Those who cannot do not develop number concepts by doing this exercise. The reason is that numbers have their source in each child's head, not in pictures of objects. This kind of exercise is based on the wrong, associationist assumption that children learn the meaning of the numeral 4 by associating it with the picture of four apples, four cookies, or four flowers. Children do not learn the meaning of a numeral through such association. They first construct the *idea* of four through their own ability to think, and then assimilate the spoken word *four* into this idea. Once the spoken word *four* is thus learned, pictures become superfluous for the learning of numerals. The numeral 4 was made to represent the spoken word *four*, not pictures of four objects.

The meaning children can get both from symbols and from signs is limited by their ability to think. This is why young children cannot understand political cartoons even when there is no writing in them. This is also why, in playing Twenty Questions, young children often ask, "Is it a dog?" after being told that the object in question is not an animal. After being told that the number to be guessed is smaller than five, they likewise often ask, "Is it eight?" While language development is important in its own right, teachers need to focus clearly on cognitive development, too.[5]

Piaget (1946/1962) showed that children assimilate reality as they engage in symbolic play. In other words, they do not come to know reality simply by being exposed to it. We can observe different levels of knowing in children's "pretend" play. Some represent only isolated bits such as "driving" and "eating," while others elaborate entire sequences with details, coherence, and even social interaction. As children think about reality in their play, their knowledge becomes more elaborate and better organized, and this higher-level knowledge is expressed in their symbolic play.[6]

Symbolic representation can also be observed in block building and a variety of art activities such as painting, drawing, and the making of models with clay, wood, and empty boxes. The teacher who knows about physical knowledge can work "science" into these art activities.[7] Following is a typical example.

---

[5]The reader interested in representation is referred to Furth (1981).

[6]Early childhood texts usually refer to symbolic play as "dramatic" play. This is an adultocentric view. Young children engage in symbolic play long before they hear about drama.

[7]This point will be clarified shortly, when I discuss how children acquire physical knowledge.

A child called Paul was trying to make a sailboat by gluing a stick perpendicularly to another piece of wood (see Figure 1). He put a small amount of glue on the end of the stick and held it up for a while. When he let go of it, it fell over. He then put more glue on the same spot, repeated the procedure, and again failed to produce the desired effect. His solution was to put even more glue on the stick and to repeat the same attempt. He could not *see* (think) that he was pushing most of the glue off the surface on which he thought he was putting more glue (see Figure 2).

Giving up trying to make a sailboat, Paul announced that he was going to make an airplane. He put glue on the side of the stick this time and laid it down lengthwise on the same piece of wood. It stayed on perfectly this time (see Figure 3). He then put glue on part of the stick (Figure 3) and laid a small plank across to make the plane's wings (Figure 4). The wings were slightly off center and fell over. His solution was to put gobs of glue on the plank and to keep replacing it on the stick until it stayed balanced.

Many kindergartens nowadays are single-mindedly teaching children to read and write letters and numerals. While these are often called "academic skills" (as if other activities were not academic), letters and numerals are only conventional graphic forms used to represent spoken language. The teaching of this social knowledge is superficial and is like trying to put icing on a cake before baking it. Such teaching may not be harmful to children who happen to be advanced for their age in cognitive development. For those who are less fortunate, however, such teaching is harmful because it limits children's mental activity and prevents them from using their time to construct the very knowledge they need to build to go on building more knowledge.

IMPLICATIONS FOR KINDERGARTEN

The implications of Piaget's theory are so vast that it is not possible to discuss all the educational goals and objectives that I derive from it. I would, therefore, like to highlight only one point — the importance of children's being mentally active. If they construct knowledge by putting things into relationships through their own mental activity, it follows that educators must try to get them to be mentally active.

As I stated in "Autonomy: The Aim of Education Envisioned by Piaget" (Kamii, 1984), autonomy is both moral and intellectual. This was the broad, long-range goal of education for Piaget. The development of moral and intellectual autonomy can be fostered by focusing more spe-

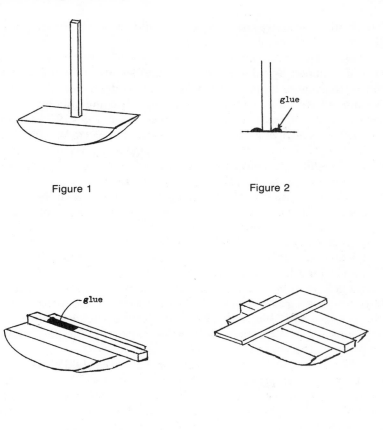

Figure 1

Figure 2

Figure 3

Figure 4

cifically on the child's relationship to adults, to other children, and to learning. These goals are:

1. That children feel secure in close relationships with adults, who reduce their power as much as possible
2. That they respect the feelings and rights of other children and co-ordinate points of view with them (decentering and negotiating)
3. That they be alert and curious, come up with interesting ideas, problems, and questions, use initiative in pursuing curiosities, have confidence in their ability to figure things out for themselves, and speak their minds with conviction

The third of the above goals is a more detailed way of saying that we want children to be mentally active.

Many kindergarten programs include the objective of children's ability to sort objects by color, shape, size, and texture. I do not endorse this objective because it does not permit children to be mentally active and because all children of normal intelligence become able to sort objects without instruction anyway (Inhelder & Piaget, 1959/1964). Below are two activities involving categories that allow children to be mentally more active than while merely sorting objects. One is a card game, which contributes to children's construction of logico-mathematical knowledge, and the other is a physical knowledge (science) activity.

The card game is called Making Families and resembles Go Fish. The cards consist of sets of four (or five or six) cards (e.g., four aces, four queens, four kings, four 5s, and four 10s), and are all dealt to three players. The first player begins by asking someone for a card, in an attempt to make a set of four of a kind and lay them down in front of him. If the person asked has the card, she has to give it. As long as the first player gets cards he asked for, he can continue asking for more. If he fails to receive the card he requested, the turn passes to the person who said, "I don't have any." Play continues until all the cards have been put down in groups of four. The person who makes more sets ("families") than anybody else is the winner.

This game involves making categories, but the child makes them not just to make them (as in a sorting activity) but to try to win cards. The game is good also because it offers the possibility of logical thinking. For example, if Mark has a king and asks Susie for one, and Susie replies that she does not have any, he can deduce that the third player must have the other three. (Kindergarten children usually do not make this deduction, and this attests to the value of this game.) The reader interested in finding out more about how this game works is referred to Kamii and DeVries (1980, chap. 10). Many other card games such as Card Dominoes can be found in the same book as well as in Kamii (1982, 1985).

The rationale for games is based partly on recent research by a group of social psychologists in Geneva who experimentally verified Piaget's claim that the exchange of viewpoints is good for children's cognitive development (Perret-Clermont, 1980; Doise & Mugny, 1984). In one of her experiments, Perret-Clermont gave fruit juice in an opaque pitcher to a nonconserver[8] and asked him to give exactly the same amount to two other

---

[8] A nonconserver is one who does not think that the quantity of water is still the same in the following task: He is first asked to pour into glass A' the same amount of liquid as is in A (of the same dimensions). The experimenter then pours the liquid in A into C, which

children to drink. The two children receiving the juice were given glasses of different shapes, one (B) being wider and shorter than the other (A). A third glass (A'), which had the same dimensions as A, was then casually given as something to use if it would be helpful. The children were told that they could drink their juice when they agreed that the two with different glasses (A and B) had exactly the same amount.

The experimental group consisted of groups of three children. They usually began by pouring the liquid into A and B. (No one used A and A' first, to transfer the content of A' into B afterwards.) The exchange of opinions continued for about 10 minutes, accompanied by many actions. For example, one child might pour some liquid from B back into the pitcher, asserting that B had more. Another might then insist on pouring some into B again to reestablish the same level. The third child might then suggest that the content of B should be emptied into A'.

Whether the group of three consisted only of nonconservers, or a nonconserver was in the majority or minority of the threesome, significantly more children in the experimental group made progress on the posttest and/or the second posttest than did those in the control group. The only difference between the control and experimental group was that the latter had the 10-minute session just described. The second posttest was given about a month after the first one. The pretest and posttests consisted of many tasks involving, for example, number, quantity of clay and liquid, and length. The benefit of sociocognitive conflict can thus be said to extend beyond the specific content of liquid in containers. The clashes among children seemed to have stimulated their ability to coordinate other relationships as well.

While logico-mathematical knowledge cannot be transmitted from other people, its construction is stimulated by the clash of ideas. Children have to think hard and critically, and coordinate viewpoints in a game, and it is this mental activity that is important for the construction of logico-mathematical knowledge. Social interaction is a major part of an educational program based on Piaget's theory, and the reader is referred to Kamii and DeVries (1977, 1980) for further details about this aspect.

The second activity that allows children to be mentally more active than the sorting of objects involves physical knowledge. A child at the

---

is a much thinner and taller glass. The child is then asked whether C has the same amount or more or less than A'.

Until the age of 7 or 8, children's thinking is preoperational, and they usually think that C has more (because the empirical information leads them to think that there is more in C than in A'). When their logic is subsequently constructed, they become able to deduce that the amount in C is the same as in A'.

water table was trying to make a unit block stay at the bottom of the water by holding it down longer and longer. After holding it down increasingly longer, she gave up on that block and went to get a longer one. She held that one down longer and longer, until she concluded that she had to get an even longer block. She tried the same action and was disgusted that the heavy, long one, too, kept springing up to the surface.

Sinking and floating are categories that depend on properties of objects, but they sometimes result from the child's action on them. For example, an empty can or the top of a jar can be made to float by being placed gently on water. But if we press down on these objects, they can be made to sink. Reality is much more complicated and ambiguous than the neat categories of "red" and "blue," and knowledge is a messy affair.

This example also shows how children construct physical knowledge. They construct it not just with their senses but by acting on objects and seeing how objects react. The senses are necessary to observe the objects' reactions, but sensory information becomes physical knowledge only in the context of the child's action, which is both physical and mental. This child acted on each block in a variety of ways to find out how the object reacted. The idea of holding the block down came from her head, and the *interpretation* of the object's reaction was also made in her head. Children thus construct logico-mathematical and physical knowledge through their own mental activity, not by being told to sort objects by color, shape, size, texture, and other obvious properties. Readers interested in knowing more about physical knowledge activities may refer to Kamii and DeVries (1978).

The kinds of initiative and experimentation described above do not just happen all by themselves. They occur only if there is a teacher who provides the materials and atmosphere that are conducive to such experimentation. While the creation of such an atmosphere is truly an art, the art of teaching ought to be based on precise scientific knowledge about how children learn. Medicine, too, is an art, but an art based on scientific knowledge, which promises to keep advancing as long as the human race goes on constructing new knowledge.

REFERENCES

Doise, W., & Mugny, G. (1984). *The social development of the intellect.* New York: Pergamon, 1984 (first published in 1981).

Furth, H. G. (1981). *Piaget and knowledge.* Chicago: University of Chicago Press.

Inhelder, B., & Piaget, J. (1958). *The growth of logical thinking from childhood to adolescence.* New York: Basic Books (first published in 1955).

Inhelder, B., & Piaget, J. (1963). De l'itération des actions à la récurrence élémentaire. In P. Gréco, B. Inhelder, B. Matalon, & J. Piaget, *La formation des raisonnements récurrentiels* (Etudes d'épistémologie génétique, XVII). Paris: Presses Universitaires de France.

Inhelder, B., & Piaget, J. (1964). *The early growth of logic in the child.* New York: Harper & Row (first published in 1959).

Kamii, C. (1982). *Number in preschool and kindergarten.* Washington, DC: National Association for the Education of Young Children.

Kamii, C. (1984). Autonomy: The aim of education envisioned by Piaget. *Phi Delta Kappan, 65,* 410–415.

Kamii, C. (1985). *Young children reinvent arithmetic.* New York: Teachers College Press.

Kamii, C., & DeVries, R. (1977). Piaget for early education. In M. C. Day & R. K. Parker (Eds.), *The preschool in action* (2nd ed.). Boston: Allyn & Bacon.

Kamii, C., & DeVries, R. (1978). *Physical knowledge in preschool education.* Englewood Cliffs, NJ: Prentice-Hall.

Kamii, C., & DeVries, R. (1980). *Group games in early education.* Washington, DC: National Association for the Education of Young Children.

Kohlberg, L., & Mayer, R. (1972). Development as the aim of education. *Harvard Educational Review, 42,* 449–498.

Locke, J. (1947). *Essay concerning human understanding.* Oxford: Oxford University Press.

McKinnon, J. W., & Renner, J. W. (1971). Are colleges concerned with intellectual development? *American Journal of Physics, 39,* 1047–1052.

Perret-Clermont, A.-N. (1980). *Social interaction and cognitive development in children.* New York: Academic Press.

Piaget, J. (1950a). *Introduction à l'épistémologie génétique: Tome 1. La pensée mathématique.* Paris: Presses Universitaires de France.

Piaget, J. (1950b). *Introduction à l'épistémologie génétique: Tome 2. La pensée physique.* Paris: Presses Universitaires de France.

Piaget, J. (1950c). *Introduction à l'épistémologie génétique: Tome 3. La pensée biologique, la pensée psychologique et la pensée sociologique.* Paris: Presses Universitaires de France.

Piaget, J. (1954). *The construction of reality in the child.* New York: Basic Books (first published in 1937).

Piaget, J. (1962). *Play, dreams, and imitation in childhood.* New York: Norton (first published in 1946).

Piaget, J. (1963). *The psychology of intelligence.* Patterson, NJ: Littlefield, Adams & Co. (first published in 1947).

Piaget, J. (1965). *The moral judgment of the child.* New York: Free Press (first published in 1932).

Piaget, J. (1966). *The child's conception of physical causality.* Totowa, NJ: Littlefield, Adams & Co. (first published in 1927).

Piaget, J. (1967). *The child's conception of the world.* Totowa, NJ: Littlefield, Adams & Co. (first published in 1926).

Piaget, J. (1969). *The child's conception of time.* London: Routledge and Kegan Paul (first published in 1946).

Piaget, J. (1970). *L'épistémologie génétique.* Paris: Presses Universitaires de France.

Piaget, J. (1971). *Biology and knowledge.* Chicago: University of Chicago Press (first published in 1967).

Piaget, J. (1975). *L'équilibration des structures cognitives.* Paris: Presses Universitaires de France.

Piaget, J. (1976). The development in children of the idea of the homeland and relations with other countries. In S. F. Campbell (Ed.), *Piaget sampler.* New York: Wiley (first published in 1951).

Piaget, J., & Inhelder, B. (1967). *The child's conception of space.* New York: Norton (first published in 1948).

Piaget, J., Inhelder, B., & Szeminska, A. (1964). *The child's conception of geometry.* New York: Harper & Row (first published in 1948).

Schwebel, M. (1975). Formal operations in first-year college students. *Journal of Psychology, 91,* 133–141.

CHAPTER 6

Play and Young Children's Learning

Olivia N. Saracho

As kindergartens have become more an accepted part of the elementary school, a feeling has developed among many educators that the kindergarten program should become more like that of the elementary school. The world of the preschool child is too often seen as a world in which children are given opportunities for play that have no significant educational or developmental consequences. Given that view, kindergarten teachers are admonished to help their children learn to put aside play and engage in work activities, often activities related to academic achievement.

In fact, play serves an important educational and developmental role in these early years. Young children, even beyond kindergarten age, continue to use play to learn about the intellectual and social world as well as the world of symbols and language. This chapter will explore what we know about play and its relationships to young children's learning.

COGNITIVE PLAY

Within the last two decades, psychologists have again become interested in the study of cognitive development, and psychology during this period has been dominated by the metaphors of cognition (e.g., information processing). The tasks of the 1980s have been (1) to incorporate the diverse strands of cognitive studies in such areas as memory, development, and social psychology, and (2) to design an applied methodology to facilitate cognitive development. One vehicle for these tasks in young children is play.

A growing body of evidence supports the importance of play as a force in young children's cognitive development (e.g., Bruner, 1972; Piaget, 1952). While correlations of playfulness with various measures of cognitive functioning show that the higher the mental age of the child, the lower the playfulness ratings (Steele, 1981), Lieberman (1965) found positive relationships between playfulness and standardized intelligence test scores. According to Lunzer (1959), the best estimate of play maturity is the degree of organization found in a child's play. Lunzer's study showed that while the organization of play behavior was not interchangeable with intelligence as a construct, the analysis of the development of behavior demonstrated a positive relationship between play maturity and intelligence. Kindergarteners exhibited more mature cognitive play behavior, while preschoolers evinced less mature cognitive play behavior (Rubin, Watson, & Jambor, 1978). The least mature level of play (functional) was negatively related to the children's capacity to classify and obtain the literal (spatial) and figurative (emphatic) point of view of other persons (Rubin & Maioni, 1975). Such a point of view is revealed when two or more children assume roles to recreate a real-life situation. For instance, some children may assume the roles of family members during the dinner meal or of fire fighters to put out a make-believe fire. These roles appear in the housekeeping and block-building areas of schools for young children (Christie, 1980, 1982).

In examining the relationship of play to the growth of logical thought, the incidence of functional (sensorimotor) and constructive play was greater than the incidence of more mature forms of play such as dramatic play and games with rules (Rubin & Maioni, 1975). When children interact with their peers, they process information that is different from what they already possess. They must consider other persons' points of view. These cognitive interactions (e.g., Siegel, Roeper, & Hooper, 1966) challenge distorted responses and bring about a state of equilibrium at a more mature level of logical thought.

A positive correlation between role taking and performance on various Piagetian tasks has also been found (Feffer, 1970; Feffer & Gourevitch, 1960), indicating that the ability to perceive the world and oneself from another's perspective requires a process of social and cognitive "decentering." Rubin and Maioni (1975) demonstrated that functional play (simple repetitive muscle movements with or without objects) correlated with performance on classification and role-taking skills, whereas dramatic play correlated with cognitive development. Children's popularity correlated with cognitive development assessed by measures of classification and seriation (Rardin & Moan, 1971) and communicative egocentrism (Deutsch, 1974). Thus, the relationship between play and cognitive development has been supported by several researchers.

These results support Piaget's (1926) assumption regarding the relationship of social interaction to cognitive development. Piaget (1962) developed three play categories based on his stages of cognitive development: (1) *practice play*, which develops during the sensorimotor stage (ages birth to 2); (2) *symbolic play*, which develops through the preoperational stage (ages 2 to 7); and (3) *games with rules*, which develop through the concrete operational stage (ages 7 to 11). Piaget interprets play as an affective-to-cognitive imbalance. He perceives symbolic play as a function of conceptual immaturity and cognitive imbalance, which is usually evident in earlier developmental stages. The caprices of the ego are expressed through symbolic play, illustrating the subservience of reality to fantasy. Rather than adapting the ego to reality, children use play to assimilate their needs and yearnings. They employ this assimilation to sustain a sense of continuity and develop a measure of ego balance, which relies on an affective component and is an essential substitute for cognitive operations. Such cognitive operations are imperative in the development of a genuine equilibrium (Piaget, 1962).

While there is much support for Piaget's theories, many researchers have examined Piaget's theory in relation to its theoretical foundations (e.g., Sutton-Smith, 1966) as well as its empirical foundations (e.g., Rosen, 1974; Singer, 1973; Smilansky, 1968). They have disputed his generalizations related to play and have criticized his omission of social and cultural variables. Beyond this, they have challenged Piaget's view of the cognitive significance of symbolic play and the lack of identification of play as an explicit cognitive function (Sutton-Smith, 1966).

Cognitive Styles

Cognitive styles identify a person's mode of understanding, thinking, remembering, judging, and solving problems. They are stylistic traits related to how individuals gain knowledge from their perceptual and intellectual experiences. One dimension of cognitive style is field dependence or independence. Field-dependent persons are sensitive to other persons. This sensitivity assists them in learning social skills. They rely primarily on externally defined goals and reinforcements. In comparison, field-independent persons tend to be socially detached. These people have strong analytic skills and prefer to establish their own standards and values. Since field-dependent children rely more heavily on authority, search for people's facial cues as a source of information, are strongly interested in people, and are sensitive to the needs of others, they acquire social skills more easily. These children may be the ones who engage more often in parallel, cooperative, or associative play. Field-independent children are more independent of authority, are socially distant, and seem to be cold and aloof. These children may be the ones who engage in solitary play.

Some researchers (e.g., Rubin, 1976; Rubin, Maioni, & Hornung,

1976; Rubin et al., 1978) have found that some children purposely engage in solitary play. Children engaged in parallel play may prefer the company of other children, while children who are able to consider other points of view may engage in associative or cooperative play (Rubin et al., 1976; Rubin, 1976). This suggests that young children's role-taking skills are less related to their involvement in parallel and solitary play than to associative play. Based on these characteristics and others provided by researchers of cognitive style (e.g., Saracho & Spodek, 1981; Saracho, 1983), a strong relationship is suggested between play and cognitive style. A number of studies have examined young children's cognitive styles and social behavior.

Children with a more field-dependent cognitive style tend to be involved in social play, while more field-independent children engage in more perceptual-motor demanding block activity. Steele (1981) found that pretend play was negatively related to cognitive style and that playfulness had a significant negative relationship with a measure of cognitive style. Aspects of these play preferences have dimensions that are probably based upon opposite directed predictions. Coates, Lord, and Jakabovics (1975) found that social orientations are displayed in play preferences related to preschool children's field-dependent cognitive functioning. Children spending more of their time playing with others were more field-dependent than those playing in relative isolation. Coates (1972) found that more preschool field-dependent girls preferred social play than did their field-independent counterparts. Significant relationships between young children's motivational and cognitive variables indicate that a longitudinal study is needed to better understand how these variables affect each other over time.

The importance of fast-moving, vigorous, high-activity behavior for the development of differences in intellectual and social behavior in young children has been examined. Social behaviors identified with preschoolers' high activity were positively correlated with verbal intelligence and field independence (Halverson & Waldrop, 1976). These results support Kagan's (1971) proposition that a stable disposition of play tempo, as indexed by variations in play activity levels, produces significant consequences in young children's social and intellectual functioning. In attempting to interpret these results, Saracho (1983) cautions that individual differences need to be considered when assessing cognitive style.

Summary

Cognitive play is recognized when children transform objects and roles in their play while simultaneously being aware of the original identity and function of the object. Young children create duality of object and role, of reality and appearance, in symbolic play. They employ an intuitive form of reversibility, performing reversible transformations that are not apparent perceptually (Piaget, 1962).

Identifying discrete play variables that demonstrate strong relationships to cognitive play can stimulate a focus in developing optimal environments for the young child's play and intellectual development. Children's growth repertoire of logical skills develops as part of the maturational process and of the changing nature of their interactions with their environment.

CREATIVE PLAY

Creative individuals develop their own interpretations, which they express through such media as art, music, and language. They disregard what is common and develop novel products. They don't copy, they invent, giving their imagination full play. Wallach and Kagan (1965) define the creative process as the development of associations that are unique and that incorporate a playful and permissive attitude. Such a definition highlights the relationship of play to creativity. In fact, research has shown that play and creativity have the same structure.

Lieberman (1965) found that young children who were more physically, cognitively, and socially spontaneous as well as more humorous and joyful were also more creative. Singer (1973) showed that children grow more creative during the ages of 3 and 4 and are able to play different kinds of imaginative games. Children's make-believe is related to their ability to concentrate for long periods of time and to enjoy their play situations. Dansky and Silverman (1973) demonstrated that children who played with materials over time were able to provide more novel responses to the objects. They concluded that play helps develop children's creative thinking. Play materials influence children's ability to create fantasy themes. Younger children are involved in less fantasy (and less of it outdoors) than are older children. The differences are related to sex, age, and the nature and location of the activity. Boys engage in more fantasy play outdoors than do girls, and with greater physical ability. Large open spaces and equipment requiring gross motor activities facilitate boys' solitary and interactive fantasy play.

Many psychologists and educators believe that the capacity to participate in pretense or fantasy play is essential to developing a wide range of cognitive and social skills (Rubin, 1980). To some degree, fantasy play relates to the development of social and cognitive skills (Bruner, 1972; Singer, 1973; Smilansky, 1968). Garvey (1977) suggests that pretense or fantasy play appears full-blown at an early age. This type of play includes voluntary transformations of the "here and now," the "you and me," and the "this and that." Garvey suggests two kinds of rules governing social pretense: (1) general procedural rules (e.g., turn-alternation rules), which become evident in the children's first year of life, and (2) situation-specific rules used in particular play episodes. Smilansky (1968) found that young children develop creative skills through sociodramatic activities. A study by Matthews, Beebe, and Bopp (1980) demonstrates that pretend play has a facilitatory influence on young children's perspective taking, that is, the ability to see things from others' points of view.

Most children's fantasy play is based on incidents in their daily lives and on day-to-day problems. Some children play "house" or other games that are very close to their real-life situations. Other children play games that may be remote from their real-life situations, through playing, for example, movie stars, Olympic athletes, cops and robbers, cowboys, or cartoon characters. In examining imaginativeness, a relationship between make-believe and the dimension of creativity may exist. Singer (1973) describes imaginativeness of play as one aspect of general creativity.

Summary

Research in developmental psychology reflects a growing interest in the functional value of young children's fantasy play. Theory development and empirical work has shown a relationship between pretend play and creativity (Matthews et al., 1980). Children's success in play depends on their capability of distinguishing cognitively between their own and another individual's points of view.

LANGUAGE PLAY

The ability to create and interpret language is one of the key elements of being human. Language allows individuals to describe objects and events abstractly. Symbols (which are employed in language) and actions and toys (which are employed in play) convey meaning of a content that is not present. Actions and toys are less abstract than language. When children first begin to represent objects and situations that are not present, their linguistic apparatus is not fully developed. Symbolic play is one of young children's ways of conveying meaning. However, being able to replicate information requires the use of language to process the difficult and expanded analysis occurring in thought (Piaget, 1962).

Both language and pretend play require the representation of reality. Children use objects (e.g., dolls for a live baby, or a piece of cloth for a doll's blanket) and words (e.g., sounds to substitute for objects) to stand for different things. Elder and Pederson (1978) found developmental differences in children's dependence on the use of objects as substitutes and in resemblance between the play object and the referent objects in play sequences. Young children go through a transition period until age 3, when the meaning of objects or actions becomes stabilized and when the activity does not require the presence of the object. Children experiment with representations and respond correctly at very low levels. Very young children seem to have difficulty defining the action, possibly because they lack clarity in representing some objects without the assistance of a concrete object.

Language is more abstract than representational play. Unlike objects, words do not resemble reality. Language also has a structure of relationships among words (i.e., rule-governed grammatical relationships). The increasing complexity in children's symbolic play helps them develop the capacity to use language to substitute for play actions or as an introduction to play rather than just as an accessory to it. This process depends in the early years on children's linguistic growth. Collective symbolism differs from symbolic play in that it is a more mature and more complex structure of play than solitary play (Piaget, 1962).

Symbolic play contributes to thought and meaning, using language and concrete objects to transmit thoughts. While, in the beginning, thoughts are expressed through objects, role playing provides a turning point in distinguishing meaning from real objects (Vygotsky, 1962). Language and symbolic systems project thought and transmit the ideas of others. Symbolic development is a uniform process relying on the reflecting cognitive development (Piaget, 1962). During group play, children project private symbolism into communicable configurations that correspond with play episodes. Thus, children develop the cognitive and language skills needed for solitary play.

Both Piaget (1962) and Vygotsky (1962) associated the appearance of symbolic play with the development of representational skills. Language facilitates social and symbolic play and games, as in playing with noises and sounds, playing with the linguistic system (e.g., spontaneously rhyming and playing with words), playing with fantasy and nonsense, and playing with conversation (Garvey, 1977). Nicolich (1977) and Fein (1979) also demonstrate a relationship between symbolic play and language development in the early years. Fein agrees with Vygotsky (1962) that language comprehension (the development of inner speech) contributes to advanced symbolic play. She also agrees with Piaget's (1962) concept that play and language serve an expressive function with very young children. Rubin and Maioni (1975) also support this relationship between symbolic play and cognitive and language development. Smilan-sky (1968) found that sociodramatic play facilitates the use of language, permitting words to replace reality. Role playing promotes social language development, the development of flexible and expressive tones, and the understanding of rules underlying the voice or conversation patterns of the role assumed.

Play is considered a spontaneous and enjoyable activity with an intrinsic goal (Garvey, 1977); the process of playing is more important than its outcome. Play functions through behavioral segments segregated from their general mediation context, which expands and integrates that behavior and provides a pleasurable effect. Children's play develops the human capacity to cope with experience through the creation of model events that allow children to conquer reality by planning and testing ideas (Erikson, 1963). Just as children build their own reality by playfully manipulating objects in the world around them, they can also build language by playfully manipulating verbal forms and meaningful communicative contexts.

Playing with language leads to literacy. During play children focus on meanings and language forms. Language structures become meaningful as children listen to language utterances and interpret meaning. Children's awareness of the rules of language is called metalinguistic awareness. Metalinguistic awareness requires exceptional cognitive demands and appears to be more universally difficult to learn than language performance, that is, speaking and listening (Cazden, 1974). The rules become the focus of the activity and meaningful contexts are automatically conveyed without focusing on them.

Typical discourse settings contain clear structural elements. During a conversation, children concentrate on transmitting a message rather than on exploring language elements. Young children use speech play, like other play forms, to explore and manipulate elements of the language structure. They initiate their participation in speech play during infancy, at first by themselves but later in social settings. Metalinguistic awareness develops as a result of speech play. As children play with language, or engage in speech play, they maniplate the phonological, syntactic, semantic, and pragmatic components of language, disregarding the traditional language goal of transmitting meaning to another (Pellegrini, 1981).

The use of newly developed resources in playful manipulation is evident in young children. Most organizational levels of language (phonology, grammar, meaning), most phenomena of speech discourse (expressive noises, variation in timing and intensity), the speakers' interactions, and the speech objectives (purpose in speaking) are potential play resources. Speech is integrated into the other play elements as an index of playful orientation, as a way of coordinating the complex activities of make-believe, and as an element in the expressive behavior or pretending. Ritualized play is constructed with the resources that language and speech provide.

Becoming aware of the language's phonological aspect presents a most important condition for developing literacy as children playfully manipulate the sounds of words separate from their meaning. They naturally utilize their capacity to learn language by employing aspects of their language as the objects of play. Children make easy transitions between clear language elements, in communicating intrapersonally, and dealing with them as opaque play objects (El'Konin, 1969).

Children provide language responses to language itself. Johnson (1928) observed that children experimented with words they heard and used, manipulating their uses and meaning as well as grammatical structure. Such experiments did not focus on meaning, value, and use but on rhythm, sounds, and form. Chukovsky (1963) noticed children initiating play with a newly acquired phase of understanding. These concepts they mastered then became toys to use in relating to reality. After age 5, children's language play consisted of puns and riddles, turning word meanings upside down, playing with the impact of dichotomous meanings simultaneously contemplated, and altering aspects of words to explore different effects.

SOCIAL PLAY

Learning to live with other people and sharing their beliefs, customs, mores, traditions, social controls, past experiences, emotions, and language are part of the process of socializing children. Young children realize that both their peers and adults have feelings, attitudes, and needs that differ from their own. Children learn a broad range of verbal and nonverbal communication skills to cope with other people's feelings, attitudes, and needs and to process information that others express or imply. They learn to sympathize with one another's feelings, to wait their turn, to cooperate with others, to share materials and experiences, and to acquire satisfaction through others. Living successfully in a society with others requires more than just being submissive to others or disregarding one's own personal needs. Children must learn to employ their own and others' resources for the purpose of sharing and cooperating. Their responses are obvious and spontaneous, making investigations natural and observable. Studies that investigate young children's behavior often conflict in theories, results, and generalizations related to social development, characteristics, and practices. There is not even an agreement on the use and meaning of the term *social*. It is often used to mean "play behavior."

Several researchers have investigated stages of children's play behavior. Parten (1932) examined the relationship between the children's age and their social play. Their social participation was classified as unoccupied, solitary play, onlooker, parallel play, group activity, associative group play, and organized supplementary group play. Social participation to a large degree depended on the children's age. The youngest children played either alone or in parallel groups, whereas older children played in more highly organized groups. Social play advanced with age, and most of the children in the study participated in parallel play.

A replication, though not identical, of Parten's study was attempted by Barnes (1971) about 40 years later. The behavior of 3- and 4-year-old children seemed to have changed substantially. Barnes stated that contemporary preschoolers had fewer skills in engaging in associative and cooperative play than did children 40 years before. Rubin et al. (1976) challenged Barnes's conclusions. Parten's study had shown that solitary and parallel play decreased between the ages of 2 and 4½ years, whereas group play increased. According to Parten's social participation measure, solitary play indicates a developmental immaturity. However, researchers (e.g., Bakeman & Brownlee, 1980; Moore, Everston, & Brophy, 1974; Rubin, 1976; Rubin et al., 1976) have recently found that solitary, parallel, and group play do not represent a simple developmental progression from immaturity to maturity. Moore and associates (1974) showed that children who were engaged in solitary play were goal-directed, indicating independent, task-oriented behavior. Solitary play was found to be a beneficial activity instead of a measure of poor social adjustment.

Rubin (1976) examined the quality of peer interaction in play and found that cooperative play rarely occurred and that solitary play was not as immature for 3- and 4-year-olds as Parten and others have indicated. Bakeman and Brownlee (1980) also questioned the assertion that parallel play is a less mature form of social play; they consider parallel play essential in children's play behavior. Their study showed that group play followed solitary play and that it is not probable that parallel play would occur. They suggest that parallel play is a social strategy rather than a developmental form and that Parten's differentiation between associative and cooperative play is probably difficult to assess (e.g., Bakeman & Brownlee, 1980; Smith, 1978). The stages of social participation for 2- and 4-year-old children seemed to be "unsocial" (unoccupied, onlooker, solitary) and "social" (parallel, associative, and cooperative) play. Fein et al. (1982) suggested that Parten's index be dichotomized to a solitary-social orientation.

In assessing the maturity of children's play, developmental progressions must be identified that are related to age and children's peer group experiences. Older children — rather than younger children — and experienced children, rather than inexperienced children, had higher attainment levels. Nicolich (1977) found that pretense play in younger children was a result of a sequential development. An integration of more elusive phases of social behavior could represent the social development of 2- to 5-year-old children.

Peer play requires children to encounter viewpoints that differ from theirs. These encounters can create difficult conditions if cognitive conflict and arousal occur. The children need to (1) assimilate other persons' points of view and reconstrue all perspectives based on their own experiences, or (2) accommodate to the distinctive perspectives by accepting many possible different modes, taking into consideration the social environment (Rubin & Hayven, 1981).

A number of studies provide evidence that peer play influences children's early social and cognitive development. Based on Piaget's (1962) concept that children's play behavior reflects their developmental level, Smilansky (1968) created four kinds of play categories analogous to Piaget's operational intellectual levels:

1. *Functional* or *sensorimotor play*, which includes simple, non-goal-oriented repetitive movements with or without objects
2. *Constructive play*, which includes the manipulation of objects as in building or creating
3. *Dramatic play*, which includes the replacement of an imaginary object or circumstance to meet their personal needs and desires
4. *Games with rules*, which includes competitive activities requiring children to accept and adapt present rules.

Both *constructive* and *dramatic play* match preoperational intelligence, while *games with rules* take effect at the beginning of the stage of concrete operations. Rubin et al. (1978) found that Smilansky's (1968) play categories are age-related. Children display less *functional* and more *dramatic play* and *games with rules* as they grow older. Rubin and Maioni's (1975) data show that play forms and cognitive development are related. Frequency of functional play exhibited during spontaneous classroom activity was negatively correlated with performance on laboratory tests of role-taking and classification skills, while dramatic play was positively correlated with cognitive skills. Using Smilansky's (1968), Piaget's (1962), and Parten's (1932) schemata, Rubin et al. (1976; 1978) included pretend play as another category. Their data showed that solitary play takes place during cognitive mature activity such as when young children construct pretensions and assume different roles.

Rubin et al.'s (1976; 1978) categories assist in modifying Parten's scale, but they do not resolve the issue of developmental progression for social cognitive classifications. Piaget's classifications may need to be narrowly refined within higher pretense levels (Fein et al., 1982).

PHYSICAL PLAY

An early childhood classroom is equipped with play materials that stimulate children to engage in a variety of actions. Several studies have shown that the physical environment has an impact on young children's behavior and an immediate psychological effect in a variety of situations.

Preschool children demonstrate negative reactions to mutilated or incomplete toys (Barker, Dembo, & Lewin, 1943). A new toy raises children's curiosity but does not necessarily sustain interest. Activities with new toys during the early part of the play period are more superficially exploratory in nature than in the later play period (Herring & Kock, 1930). Preschool children explore materials of high realism — realistic miniature furniture and bendable dolls appropriately dressed — to a greater extent than materials of low realism — crudely constructed, blocklike furniture and sexless stuffed dolls without clothing (Phillips, 1945). Play materials vary greatly in the uniformity of their appeal to groups. High-structure play objects (e.g., tea set, stove, sink combination, refrigerator, ironing board, dolls) increase the frequency of noninteractive pretend play in 3½-year-old triads (three children playing together) but not in 5-year-old triads. This seems to conflict with Piaget's (1962) belief that young children's pretend play is only minimally related to adjustments to the physical environment. Both 3- and 5-year-old triads were receptive to the functional ambiguity of low-structure play objects (pipe cleaners, cardboard boxes, metal cans, construction paper, styrofoam cups, paper bags, blocks) and increased the incidence of substitutions. Children were aware of and receptive to critical variations between the two kinds of play objects in the physical environment.

Studies investigating the children's choices for the various play materials also indicated that the materials differ in appeal to individual children. Bott (1928) found that children (ages 2 and 5) had distinct preferences for particular toys based on their age. Younger children played a long time with beans, while older children played with jigsaw puzzles. Van Alstyne (1932/1976) found that the most popular materials for 2- to 5-year-olds were blocks, clay, and a doll corner. Bott (1928) found that children of all ages preferred such toys as small mechanical toys, peg-boards, sectional trains, and beans.

Even though the quality and quantity of play and the endurance of interest in these play materials varied between younger and older children, trucks ranked highest in attractiveness and the merit of ascending order for other toys including tops, acorns, tinker toys, and books (Herring & Kock, 1930). Blocks were the first choice of play materials with more popularity and social value. Other play materials that were selected included sand, a house corner, kiddy cars, and a seesaw, while those which were hardly ever selected included a blackboard, animals, and dolls. Van Alstyne (1932/1976) found that, when the duration of time spent was examined, the interest decreased from 2- to 5-year-olds in the doll corner and easel painting, and increased for blocks, crayons, and balls; interest remained approximately the same for scissors and clay.

Children's choices of play materials were examined using the same children at different ages (3 and 4). The results showed that at 3, children preferred cylinders, bricks, and color pairs. While cylinders were the most popular, children did not play with them for a long period of time. At 4, children preferred making simple patterns by tracing around the metal insets with colored crayons. Other popular choices for 3s were the Montessori cylinders, color matching, and large bricks; while 4s preferred the Montessori dressing frames, cylinders, metal insets for tracing, wooden insets, and colored cubes. Least popular choices for 3s were the Montessori pink tower, sweeping with brush and pan, lacing material in frames, and playing with stuffed animals and a china tea set. The 4s' least popular choices were inset cards (which were never used), placing numbers against counting rods, word building, drawing with crayons, and chalking on the board (Bridges, 1927; 1929).

Summary

Play materials serve specific functions during the child's development. The way the play materials are used varies for the different age groups (Kawin, 1934; Westby, 1980). Play development is a gradual, continuous process. What toys are preferred and how they are used depend on the child's age. Play materials accommodate themselves to a large number of different experiences. Although they can be classified in many different ways, children's ages serve as a general guide in selecting toys.

Play materials can be classified into several distinct categories, each meeting a different need in play life and development. The early childhood classroom usually includes miniature representations of the objects of life around children (e.g., dolls, doll furniture, wagons, engines). Such toys elicit role taking or dramatizations of the serious and meaningful experiences of adults. These toys offer children some of the knowledge as well as the meaning and the standards and skills incorporated in the domestic and industrial experiences of the world around young children. They help children to understand life, to assume the roles of others, and to understand the feelings of others. Skills that coordinate the senses and muscles can be taught through such toys as hoops, tops, balls, slides, seesaws, and swings.

Children learn to produce valuable and aesthetically pleasing objects, using artistic and literary play materials such as pictures and books. Toys should be considered as more than artistic ornaments or mechanical aspects, while books and pictures should be used to motivate intellectual or aesthetic play. The specific stage of young children's physical development must be considered in selecting play materials that will promote their development. Play materials that facilitate the teaching of specific skills or concepts for planned activities are considered most valuable.

EDUCATIONAL IMPLICATIONS

Play exhibits the primacy of assimilation over accommodation, allowing it to transform reality into its own mode without yielding that transformation to the criterion of objective reality. Play avoids becoming subservient to accommodative imitation from the moment that sensorimotor play becomes symbolic. Westby (1980) has described symbolic play stages based on the findings and theories of several experts on play. This is summarized as follows:

Stage I: Children (9–12 months) cultivate object permanence and are able to find hidden toys. They use the toy appropriately with some formative vocalizations.

Stage II: Children (13–17 months) explore toys, immediately find the part of the toy that is responsible for its operation (levers, strings, switches, buttons), and test several motor schemata (pushing, pulling, turning, pounding, shaking). Some children speak single words, which are complex, context-dependent, and unstable. Children try to have a more purposeful communication and employ gestures and vocalizations in requesting, commanding, attracting attention, interacting, greeting, protesting, and labeling.

Stage III: Children (17–19 months) display the beginnings of representational capacities. They participate in symbolic play, are able to discover hidden toys, and initiate a true verbal language, indicating a marked growth in the number of words that they employ.

Stage IV: Children (19–22 months) expand their symbolism to include other actors or receivers of action. They employ word combinations that have a variety of semantic relations. Since they have internalized action schemata, they are able to refer to objects and individuals in their absence.

Stage V: Children (24 months) assume roles using pretend toys that are realistic in appearance and close to life-size. They describe their actions with sentences and are able to use present progressing *-ing* markers on verbs as well as plural and possessive word endings. Their communicative performances are extended in pretending, sharing information, and questioning, even though they may not utilize syntactic question forms.

Stage VI: Children (2½ years) initiate representations of situations that are less frequently experienced or observed, especially those which are impressive or traumatic. They need realistic props. The roles they assume shift immediately, and the situations are short and isolated. They employ language selectively in analyzing their views. They tend to ask "Why?" questions, especially in reaction to negative statements made by an adult, although the child may not listen to the response. Parallel play predominates, and associative play becomes apparent.

Stage VII: Children (3 years) continue the role-playing activities of Stages V and VI, although now they associate a number of schemas to one another in a sequence. They still rely on realistic props. Associative play is evident, but cooperative play appears. They re-enact previous situations by creating outcomes based on the children's wishes.

Stage VIII: Children (3½ years) assume roles using less realistic toys, such as blocks, to represent houses, barns, or fences. They are able to consider another person's point of view and have the metalinguistic capacity to think about language and comment on it. Children give toys dialogue, as when they give a doll a personality to engage while playing.

Stage IX: Children (4 years) hypothesize future events and verbalize them. They begin to use modals and conjunctions but have not achieved full competence with these linguistic concepts. They use toys in a more elaborate form, such as three-dimensional block structures, or elaborate with dolls and puppets to create entire scenes of an event.

Stage X: Children (5 years) are role-playing in advance events involving other children and several objects. They coordinate more than one situation taking place at the same time. They do not need realistic props but use their imagination to create the scenes. Cooperative play is evident. They are able to employ time-relational terms such as *then, when, first, while, next, before*, and *after*. The modals and conjunctions of Stage IX will not be used with full competence with such terms until they reach the age of twelve. Children can be almost nonverbal but still display play behavior until Stage IX. In Stage X, the children's play behavior shows that children use language (signed or spoken) effectively to organize the situation.

While these stages have not been validated by research, they provide an integrative summary of the cognitive, creative, language, social, and physical elements of play.

Research provides evidence that there is a relationship between play and learning. Play helps young children understand the world. Teachers can become facilitators of learning through play by being supportive and indirect in their teaching. Specific forms of play and learning activities range from activities requiring minimal adult intervention to activities that are highly structured by adults.

The studies reviewed provide a knowledge base about children's play, which can be associated with theories of early childhood development and learning (such as those suggested by Piaget or Bruner). Educators who become aware of these relationships are able to suggest teaching strategies for incorporating play in their teaching. Since play is difficult to define and research outcomes often conflict or lack clarity, teachers need to be careful not to misinterpret the value of play and view it as having meager practical utility. Teachers must identify their educational goals and then look for play alternatives as they plan. They must become keen observers and evaluators of educational goals, intervening in children's activities in relation to their play to make it more potent.

Teachers must become sensitive to the learning generated through a play curriculum. Such a curriculum allows teachers to engage in socializing and preparing young children for the world of family- and work-related adult roles. They need to be aware of the body of knowledge that exists about education and play and to communicate it to colleagues, supervisors, and parents. Such knowledge is also necessary in order to make worthwhile decisions in planning a play curriculum.

REFERENCES

Bakeman, R., & Brownlee, J. R. (1980). The strategic use of parallel play: A sequential analysis. *Child Development, 51*, 873–878.
Barker, R. B., Dembo, L., & Lewin, L. (1943). Frustration and regression: An

experiment with young children. In R. R. Barker, J. S. Kounin, & H. F. Wright (Eds.), *Child behavior and development*, (pp. 441–458). New York: McGraw-Hill.

Barnes, K. E., (1971). Preschool play norms: A replication. *Development Psychology, 5,* 99–103.

Bott, N. (1928). Observation of play activities in a nursery school. *Genetic Psychology Monographs, 4,* 44–88.

Bridges, K. M. B. (1927). Occupational interests of three-year-old children. *Journal of Genetic Psychology, 34,* 415–423.

Bridges, K. M. B. (1929). The occupational interests of attention of four-year-old children. *Pedagogical Seminary and Journal of Genetics Psychology, 36,* 551–570.

Bruner, J. S. (1972). Nature and use of immaturity. *American Psychologist, 27,* 687–708.

Cazden, C. B. (1974). Play with language and metalinguistic awareness: One dimension of language experience. *International Journal of Early Childhood, 6,* 12–24.

Christie, J. F. (1980). Play for cognitive growth. *Elementary School Journal, 81,* 115–118.

Christie, J. F. (1982). Sociodramatic play training. *Young Children, 37*(4), 25–32.

Chukovsky, K. (1963). *From two to five* (M. Morton, Trans.). Berkeley: University of California Press.

Coates, S. (1972). *The preschool embedded figures test — PEFT.* Palo Alto, CA: Consulting Psychologists Press.

Coates, S., Lord, M., & Jakabovics, E. (1975). Field dependence-independence, social-nonsocial play, and sex differences in preschool children. *Perceptual and Motor Skills, 40,* 195–202.

Dansky, J. L., & Silverman, I. W. (1973). Effects of play on associative fluency in preschool-aged children. *Developmental Psychology, 9,* 38–43.

Deutsch, F. (1974). Observational and sociometric of peer popularity and their relationship to egocentric communication in female preschoolers. *Developmental Psychology, 10,* 745–747.

Elder, J. L., & Pederson, D. R. (1978). Preschool children's use of objects in symbolic play. *Child Development, 49,* 500–504.

El'Konin, D. B. (1969). Some results of the study of the psychological development of preschool-age children. In M. Cole & I. Maltzman (Eds.), *A handbook of contemporary Soviet psychology*, (pp. 215–242). New York: Basic Books.

Erikson, E. J. (1963). *Childhood and society.* New York: Norton.

Feffer, M. A. (1970). Developmental analysis of interpersonal behavior. *Psychological Review, 77,* 197–214.

Feffer, M. A., & Gourevitch, V. (1960). Cognitive aspects of role-taking in children. *Journal of Personality, 28,* 383–396.

Fein, G. G. (1979). Echoes from the nursery: Piaget, Vygotsky, and the relationship between language and plan. *New Directions in Child Development, 6,* 1–14.

Fein, G. G., Moorin, E. R., & Enslein, J. (1982). Pretense and peer behavior: An intersectoral analysis. *Human Development, 25,* 392–406.

Garvey, C. (1974). Some properties of social play. *Merrill-Palmer Quarterly, 20*(3), 163–180.

Garvey, C. (1977). *Play.* Cambridge: Harvard University Press.

Halverson, C. F., & Waldrop, M. F. (1976). Relations between preschool activity and aspects of intellectual and social behavior at age 7½. *Developmental Psychology, 12*(2), 107–112.

Herring, A., & Kock, L. H. (1930). A study of some factors influencing the interest span of preschool children. *Pedagogical Seminary and Journal of Genetic Psychology, 38,* 249–279.

Johnson, H. M. (1928). *Children in the nursery school.* New York: Day.

Kagan, J. (1971). *Change and continuity in infancy.* New York: Wiley.

Kawin, E. (1934). The function of toys in relation to child development. *Childhood Education, 11*(3), 122–133.

Lieberman, J. N. (1965). Playfulness and divergent thinking: An investigation of their relationship at the kindergarten level. *Journal of Genetic Psychology, 107,* 219–224.

Lunzer, E. A. (1959). Intellectual development in the play of young children. *Educational Review, 11*(3), 205–217.

Matthews, W. S., Beebe, S., & Bopp, M. (1980). Spatial perspective-taking and pretend play. *Perceptual and Motor Skills, 5*(1), 49–50.

Moore, N. V., Everston, C. M., & Brophy, J. E. (1974). Solitary play: Some functional reconsiderations. *Developmental Psychology, 10*(6), 830–834.

Nicolich, L. M. (1977). Beyond sensorimotor intelligence: Assessment of symbolic maturity through analysis of pretend play. *Merrill-Palmer Quarterly, 23,* 89–99.

Parten, M. B. (1932). Social participation among pre-school children. *Journal of Abnormal and Social Psychology, 27*(3), 243–269.

Pellegrini, A. D. (1981). Speech play and language development in young children. *Journal of Research and Development in Education, 14*(3), 75–80.

Phillips, R. (1945). Doll play as a function of the realism of the materials and the length of the experimental session. *Child Development, 16,* 145–166.

Piaget, J. (1926). *The language and thought of the child.* London: Routledge and Kegan Paul.

Piaget, J. (1952). *The origins of intelligence.* New York: International Press.

Piaget, J. (1962). *Play, dream, and imitation in childhood.* New York: Norton.

Rardin, D. R., & Moan, C. E. (1971). Peer interaction and cognitive development. *Child Development, 42,* 1685–1699.

Rosen, C. E. (1974). The effects of sociodramatic play on problem-solving behavior among culturally disadvantaged preschool children. *Child Development, 45,* 920–927.

Rubin, K. H. (1976). Relation between social participation and role-taking skill in preschool children. *Psychological Reports, 39,* 823–826.

Rubin, K. H. (1980). Fantasy play: Its role in the development of social skills and social cognition. *New Directions for Child Development*, 9, 69–84.

Rubin, K. H., & Hayven, M. (1981). The social and cognitive play of preschool-aged children differing with regard to sociometric status. *Journal of Research and Development in Education*, 14(3), 116–121.

Rubin, K. H., Maioni, T. L., & Hornung, M. (1976). Free-play behaviors in middle- and low-class preschoolers: Parten and Piaget revisited. *Child Development*, 47, 414–419.

Rubin, K. H., & Maioni, T. L. (1975). Play preferences and its relationship to egocentrism, popularity and classification skills in preschoolers. *Merrill-Palmer Quarterly*, 21(3), 171–179.

Rubin, K. H., Watson, K. S., & Jambor, T. W. (1978). Free play behaviors in preschool and kindergarten children. *Child Development*, 49, 534–536.

Saracho, O. N. (1983). Assessing individual differences in young children. *Studies in Educational Evaluation*, 18, 229–236.

Saracho, O. N., & Spodek, B. (1981). Teachers' cognitive styles and their educational implications. *Educational Forum*, 45(2), 153–159.

Siegel, I. C., Roeper, A., & Hooper, F. H. (1966). A training procedure for the acquisition of Piaget's conversation of quantity: A pilot study and its replication. *British Journal of Educational Psychology*, 36, 301–311.

Singer, J. L. (1973). *The child's world of make-believe.* New York: Academic Press.

Smilansky, S. (1968). *The effects of sociodramatic play on disadvantaged preschool children.* New York: Wiley.

Smith, P. K. (1978). A longitudinal study of social participation in preschool children: Solitary and parallel play re-examined. *Developmental Psychology*, 14, 517–523.

Steele, C. (1981). Play variables as related to cognitive constructs in three- to six-year-olds. *Journal of Research and Development in Education*, 14(3), 58–72.

Sutton-Smith, B. (1966). Piagetian play: A critique. *Psychological Review*, 73, 104–110.

Van Alstyne, D. (1976). *Play behavior and choice of play materials of preschool children.* New York: Arno Press (first published in 1932).

Vygotsky, L. S. (1962). *Thought and language.* Cambridge: MIT Press.

Wallach, M. A., & Kagan, N. (1965). *Modes of thinking in young children: A study of the creativity-intelligence distinction.* New York: Holt, Rinehart and Winston.

Westby, C. E. (1980). Assessment of cognitive and language abilities through play. *Language, Speech, and Hearing Services in Schools*, 11, 154–168.

CHAPTER 7

Socialization in the Kindergarten Classroom

Shirley G. Moore

At 5 years of age, give or take a year, children in our society go to school. Most preschoolers have already been introduced to the peer group, either formally, through their participation in nursery school programs or enrollment in out-of-home child care, or informally, through neighborhood peer associations. Nevertheless, entrance to the elementary school marks a turning point in the child's social and intellectual life. At that point the child enters a cohesive social system to which he or she will belong for many years to come. The school is the major social unit outside of the home where the child must adapt to be considered "competent" and "adjusted."

The school classroom can be viewed as a miniculture — a Kinder Society as it were — in which the individuals in the social system become well acquainted with one another, are interdependent, and share goals and values that govern the activities of the group. The teacher is the prime authority in the classroom, biasing the system toward an autocracy (children do not vote their teacher into power) rather than a democracy. Nevertheless, the school classroom in our society is seen by many educators as a place where children prepare themselves to live in a democracy. They become literate so that they can participate in the governance of the larger society, they acquire the skills necessary to compete in the marketplace, and they learn the social values of the culture, including abiding by the rules of the group and recognizing that individuals have rights and deserve fair treatment. Even 5-year-olds are expected to acquire a sense of responsibility to the group that goes with the privilege of membership.

The extent to which the kindergarten classroom can provide children with a positive sense of membership in a peer society will depend on the morale of the classroom, the caring and civility displayed by the participants, the support teachers and students can give each other even as the children compete and strive for individual excellence, and the extent to which the group can establish cooperative goal structures that enhance individual self-esteem without causing invidious social comparison.

Children entering the kindergarten classroom are immediately cast into two social roles that are significantly different from roles they have assumed during their earlier years of adaptation to the family. One role is that of *group member* in a society of age-mates. The other is the role of *student*. A child is almost certainly advantaged by having had some exposure to both of these social roles, for example, by having had extensive peer group play experiences and by having had parents who recognized that the child has been a "learner" from birth on. Nevertheless, the roles of group member and student in the school classroom are considerably more institutionalized than previous roles the child has experienced. The protocol governing role behavior and role relationships in the kindergarten is more likely to be determined by the larger issues of educational philosophy and school tradition than by the idiosyncrasies of fifteen to twenty five 5-year-olds from that many different homes.

In the discussion that follows, three topics will be given consideration. First, attention will be given to some basic aspects of the adult-child relationship that have particular significance for teachers as they carry out their job of introducing children to the culture of the school. Next, the two psychological-social roles to be mastered by children in school — *group member* and *student* — will be examined in some detail. Attention will be given to the skills and competencies that 5-year-olds bring to the school experience and to the teacher's role in preparing the child to meet the demands of the school. Although a complete treatment of techniques used by adults to teach and guide young children is beyond the scope of this chapter, suggestions will be made along the way regarding classroom practice.

ADULT-CHILD INTERACTION: STRATEGIES AND PROCESSES

In considering the role of adults in the socialization of young children, some selected adult-child interaction behaviors and processes will be addressed. For purposes of this chapter, the processes addressed will be those of importance in the establishment of *prosocial behavior*, friendly interaction with adults and peers and consideration for others; and *school responsibility*, compliance with adult authority figures, achievement behavior, and a predisposition to work cooperatively with others on common goals. Less attention will be given to socialization strategies involved in the control of disruptive or aggressive behavior.

Five socialization strategies appear to have particular relevance for the acquisition of (and preference for) responsible prosocial behaviors in children during the early years of life. Two strategies, the use of *positive social reinforcement* and the infusion of *nurturance* into adult-child relationships, are thought to be particularly important in securing the affectional bond between an adult and a child that predisposes the child to *want* to please the adult. Three additional strategies add important cognitive-instructional components to the adult-child relationship: *modeling acceptable behavior, providing clear expectancies and standards for behavior*, and *character attribution*. Although these socialization strategies have been explored more fully in the parent-child relationship than in teacher-child interactions, their relevance for any environment in which children and adults interact on an ongoing basis has been documented in observations in homes and schools as well as in experimental laboratory settings. Each of the five socialization strategies identified above will be given some attention in the ensuing discussion.

Positive Social Reinforcement

One of the most thoroughly documented phenomena in adult-child relationships is that contingent positive reinforcement from adults facilitates the acquisition of new behaviors in the child's repertoire and increases the probability of the occurrence of behaviors already established. Contingent social reinforcement in the form of smiles, affectionate pats or hugs, a compliment, or some other indicator of approval or appreciation appears to increase the occurrence of friendly interaction, considerateness, achievement striving, attentiveness, involvement, initiative, cooperation, and compliance. This is not to say that children are unimpressed with material rewards such as money, prizes, and tokens of success for these things. They are, of course, but because of the particular significance of adults from the earliest months of life on, young children are highly responsive to social reinforcement from parents and teachers. Furthermore, during a period of adjustment to new experiences or a new environment, reinforcement from adults serves as an important cue to the child as to precisely which behaviors, of all those that might be displayed, are valued in the new situation. This is particularly important in helping children to adapt to the kindergarten classroom. For the most part, children entering a classroom will "have their antennae out" for indicators of which behaviors will be rewarded and appreciated in this setting and which will be discouraged or ignored. Of course, there are limits to the power of social reinforcement (some of which will be commented on below) but in all probability no single factor in the teacher-child relationship will carry more of the burden of establishing appropriate behavior in the classroom than the generous use of positive social reinforce-

ment from teachers for behaviors they wish their students to display.
Unfortunately, busy teachers can slip into the pattern of having their
own "antennae out" for misbehavior rather than for good behavior, taking good behavior for granted. Behavior analysts addressing this issue have
occasionally taken the position that teachers should simply ignore misbehavior, attending as much as possible to only those behaviors they wish
to encourage (Harris, Wolf, & Baer, 1967). Although the rationale for
this suggestion (that behavior is encouraged by *negative* as well as by
positive attention) is highly questionable except in the case of children
who are really "doing battle" with authority figures, the strategy itself
is worth considering, since appropriate behaviors that get positive attention from adults tend to "squeeze out" and gradually replace inappropriate behaviors that fail to get attention — positive or negative — from
adults.

Ironically, there is some evidence to suggest that teachers are less conscientious about rewarding the good behavior of problem children than
they are about rewarding the good behavior of well-behaved children.
In a discussion of this curious state of affairs with a group of early childhood teachers attending a Minneapolis workshop, three reasons were offered to explain the phenomenon. First, difficult children have to be
reminded so often about their behavior that when they behave well,
teachers are more likely to attribute the behavior to their own effort and
persistence rather than to the child's compliance — and we do not ordinari-
ly compliment a child for performing a behavior that we have just had
to insist on! Second, teachers felt that difficult children already get more
than their share of attention for their misbehavior; they tended not to
notice these children unless they felt misbehavior was imminent. Finally, the acceptable behaviors of difficult children presumably occur with
less frequency than such behaviors of other children; hence it requires
more vigilance on the part of the teacher to notice and reward them. The
teachers offering these insights were not aware of their biases in rewarding children's good behavior. Although the reasons for their actions are
understandable, their patterns of reinforcement were probably counterproductive for problem children. They also recognized that rectifying the
situation was more a matter of orientation than of time allotment, since
showing approval or offering a compliment takes but a few seconds and
does not usually require an interruption of ongoing activities.

Some words of caution are in order at this point regarding the use
of social reinforcement in the classroom. First, rewards should not be
given to children frivolously or thoughtlessly, so that they lose their meaning as indicators of achievement. Showering children with praise and approval for tasks that are easy and require little effort may actually reduce
the effectiveness (and the discriminant value) of rewards in motivating

children to strive for appropriate levels of performance, levels commen-
surate with their abilities.

A related point is that reinforcement should be calibrated to the level
of mastery shown by the child. Behavior analysts describe a procedure
called "successive approximation" in which an unskilled (or unmotivated)
child is rewarded for a relatively poor performance during the early stages
of learning or skill acquisition. As the child's performance improves,
however, reinforcement would no longer be given for minimal accomplishments — instead the child would be applauded for achievement closer
to the cutting edge of his or her new ability. During the process of mastery, the child should be generously encouraged to show effort and persistence in moving toward a goal.

Recent research on motivation in learning also indicates that external reinforcement (material or social rewards given by adults) can undermine a child's motivation when it is given for a task that the child is
already highly motivated to perform out of intrinsic interest (Lepper,
Greene, & Nisbett, 1973). Lepper and his coworkers demonstrated that
children can actually be led to underestimate their interest in a task by
attributing their own motivation to the external rewards. Even if attribution is not involved, however, external rewards may distract children from
experiencing the personal satisfaction of completing a task. Also, the child
may come to expect external rewards for all tasks and feel cheated when
they are not forthcoming.

Finally, although there is little empirical evidence to support this
proposition, successful teachers appear to be generous with *noncontingent*
as well as *contingent* reinforcement. They convey in many different ways
their pleasure in having a child be a part of their class, unrelated to conformity or to specific accomplishments. It is natural for a teacher to greet,
with a smile and a kind word, the arrival each morning of an enthusiastic,
cooperative child, whereas a child who spells trouble and will need management throughout the day may be ignored despite the fact that the
payoff for encouragement to that child (who does not *earn* much approval) may be considerable. Young children who are used to being "in
trouble" are often extremely impressed with a smile, a kind word, or a
privilege; it primes the child to face the day with a clean slate and some
hope for a better outcome than on other days.

Nurturance

Nurturance in adult-child relationships enhances the impact that
adults have on children. Children particularly enjoy, admire, and willingly cooperate with adults who are supportive and considerate compared

with adults who are hostile, autocratic, and power-assertive (Becker, 1964; Maccoby & Martin, 1983). In the 1940s and 1950s, when the social learning processes involved in child rearing were the subject of investigation, a style of "psychological discipline" was identified that incorporated heavy doses of nurturance into the parent-child relationship combined with nonphysical punishment that stressed parental hurt feelings and disappointment (Sears, Maccoby, & Levin, 1957). The combination was particularly powerful in arousing guilt and anxiety in children, eliciting conformity, strengthening resistance to temptation, and encouraging restitution. Although teachers do not have as dependent and intense a relationship with a child in the classroom as parents do, young children become very fond of their teachers—especially warm, nurturant teachers. One would have to suspect that mild forms of psychological discipline from nurturant teachers would be effective for most children.

Of course, children do have less to fear from a nurturant authority figure than from a strict one; sanctions against misbehavior are less severe, and forgiveness is more readily forthcoming. Consequently, teachers wishing to establish a basically nurturant relationship with students would do well also to convey to the children clear expectations and behavioral goals so that their motivation to measure up to reasonable standards is not undermined. In the social learning child-rearing literature, a parent who is supportive and generous with affection but also holds the child to high standards of behavior was called a "benevolent autocrat." In the extreme, this combination of psychological discipline and high standards was too anxiety-arousing for many children, since the child had so much to lose in the loss of support from a highly nurturant parent yet constantly had to measure up to high standards to maintain the support. Clearly, adults need to be sensitive to cues from children as to when discipline is making a child overly anxious and compliant. For most kindergarten children (although not all, of course) a little disapproval from their teacher goes a long way in eliciting conformity. In fact, some children are so sensitive to adult authority that just witnessing stern disapproval of the more robust children in a group frightens them into anxious overcompliance.

Modeling and the Process of Identification

A third technique for influencing human behavior is modeling. Children tend to imitate the behavior of others, particularly competent others, in virtually all situations to which they must adapt. The effectiveness of adult models in direct teaching has been demonstrated, as in the case of teaching children to count, to use a pair of scissors, or to swim. However, the role of adult models in teaching social skills in general, and responsible prosocial behavior in particular, appears to involve a more subtle process of identification rather than the commonplace process of imitation. Children who have close associations with powerful, affectionate adults tend to identify with those adults, emulating not only their behaviors but their values, affective responses, gestures, and attitudes. Furthermore, the child takes special pleasure in matching the behavior of a revered model. One of the significant differences between the concept of *imitation* as it is incorporated into social learning accounts of modeling and *identification* as it is used in psychoanalytic and other dynamic personality theories is that identification is accompanied by high affect and investment in the match between one self and another. As children form a stable concept of the self, they become conscious of their efforts to be like selected models. They do not just imitate them; they try to think and behave as they believe the model would think and behave in their place.

Two of the characteristics that appear to facilitate a child's identification with significant adults is power (that which is almost routinely invested in adults vis-à-vis children) and a nurturant affectionate bond (that which must be earned by the adult). A hostile rejecting relationship between a child and a very powerful adult may, in fact, culminate in the child's forming what might be called a "negative identification" — at all costs, be different! (Although the concept of negative identification has intuitive appeal, there is no direct empirical evidence for such a phenomenon.)

Adults model, through their own behavior, their degree of commitment (or lack of it) to the values they attempt to teach children. Teaching one social value while demonstrating another is likely to cause the child to miss or ignore the message. Martin Hoffman's studies of child rearing elaborate this point (Hoffman, 1963). He found that parents who attempted to teach their children "consideration for others" by instructing them to behave in ways consistent with that value were most successful when they also demonstrated the value in their own interactions with their children — by, for example, using threats and force sparingly, listening to the child's point of view on an issue, and giving reasons and explanations for demands placed on the child. Case studies of altruism suggest a similar modeling effect. In a study of civil rights leaders of the 1960s, for example, degree of commitment was predicted by the extent to which civil rights workers' parents before them had been committed to similar causes of their day — and conveyed their social values to their children (Rosenhan, 1969).

Teachers would do well to deliberately model the role of "student" regularly for their children. Young children take for granted the intellectual competence of adults and do not seem to realize that adults have learned much of what they know by reading books and newspapers, watching educational TV, and consulting experts. Teachers should willingly plead ignorance when they lack knowledge, display their own intellectual curiosity, and remain alert for opportunities for their children to teach *them* something.

Demands and Expectations

Another factor in adult-child relations that appears to be important in teaching social and academic responsibility is the extent to which adults clearly convey their expectations to their children and place appropriate demands on them for compliance. Diana Baumrind (1971), in her studies of social responsibility, found that parents who expected responsible behavior from their sons and rewarded it when it occurred had sons who took more responsibility than the sons of parents who were highly permissive regarding social responsibility. In an earlier study of child rearing, Baldwin (1948) described a similar finding in which parents who used "democratic" child-rearing techniques (allowing the child to express his or her view) coupled with moderate-to-high levels of control over the child had children who were more responsible than the children of parents who used *either* democratic techniques or control without the other. Finally, Hoffman (1963), in the previously mentioned child-rearing studies, found that parents who used "consequence-oriented" disciplinary techniques, in which children were made aware of the negative impact of their misbehavior on others, were more likely than other children to apologize or make restitution for their transgressions.

Children in school also benefit from clear indicators from their teachers of what is expected of them. Young children may need more reminders and more time to learn the classroom protocol than older children, but for most of them, the ability to regulate and control their own behavior will be facilitated by explicit (albeit gentle) messages from teachers as to what is acceptable and unacceptable social behavior in the classroom.

Adult expectations regarding achievement behavior also appear to affect children's motivation and performance on tasks requiring cognitive effort. Studies of mother-child interaction during the first years of life indicate correlational relations between early competence and maternal or care giver behaviors, such as social and verbal stimulation; time spent in social interaction and adult-child play; responsiveness to infant distress signals; encouragement for exploration and initiative; offering a secure base of support for the child during exploration; valuing achievement and persistence; providing intellectually stimulating experiences, such as excursions outside the home; exposing the child to toys and other materials that facilitate concept development; and providing books and age-appropriate games (Maccoby & Martin, 1983; Yarrow, Rubenstein, & Pederson, 1972; Kagan & Moss, 1962).

Performance in academic cognitive achievement situations has also been affected by intervention programs for high-risk children under 6. Considering the long-term follow-up assessments of the compensatory education programs of the 1960s and 1970s (Head Start, Home Start, and similar funded projects), good-quality programs appear to have been successful in helping a significant number of high-risk children to enter the school system better prepared to meet its demands. Despite the fact that many of these children continued to flounder academically along the way, overall, children from early childhood programs (representing many different educational strategies, from highly structured programs to "open-classroom" models) stayed in school longer, were less likely to be placed in special education classrooms, and were less likely to fail a grade than similar children who had not participated in the intervention programs (Consortium for Longitudinal Studies, 1983; Weikart, 1983).

There would seem to be little doubt that parents, care givers, and early childhood teachers who provide children with stimulating learning opportunities and who support achievement behavior are motivated by the belief that these opportunities will contribute to the child's intellectual development. The beliefs and expectations carried in the minds of the adults may be every bit as important as the specific activities they provide. Ironically, evidence suggests that when high-risk children get into the elementary school, the contrast between their readiness and the readiness of middle-class children leads teachers to have low expectancies for them. In this regard, research on teacher behaviors based on expectancies is most revealing.

In the classic study *Pygmalion in the Classroom* by Rosenthal and Jacobson (1968) teachers' beliefs about the competencies of their students were self-fulfilling prophecies in that teachers treated children differently as a function of those beliefs, contributing to the maintenance of the academic differences. Classroom observations have confirmed that good students are given more opportunities to participate, more time to respond, and are praised more for correct answers and criticized less for incorrect responses than poor students. Teachers also are inclined to attribute the poor performance of good students to lack of effort, whereas they attribute the poor performance of weaker students to lack of ability despite the fact that poor students often lack the persistence and motivation to work hard. Undoubtedly teachers are correct much of the time in their attributions, but the total effect may be to fail to challenge the poor student. Teachers' bias in the treatment of good students and marginal students is sometimes presented as though it were a sinister plot on the part of teachers against low socioeconomic or minority students. In fact, most of their behaviors are consistent with attempts to keep classroom instruction peppy and interesting and to protect poor students from further failure and embarrassment. Nevertheless, in the process of doing so, they may be reducing opportunities for these children to do their best and conditioning them to accept failure.

A similar phenomenon is evident in the differential treatment of boys and girls by teachers. Teachers are inclined to attribute poor performance in boys to lack of effort, admonishing them to try harder, whereas they more often attribute poor performance in girls to lack of ability, accepting the performance as the best the child can do. Inasmuch as boys and girls do not come to school with different levels of preparation or different academic ability, the biases in this case do not reflect actual differences.

Attribution

In a discussion of child-rearing research, Radke-Yarrow, Zahn-Waxler, and Chapman (1983) identified a parenting technique of particular importance in getting children to perform responsible, considerate, and unselfish behaviors. These investigators referred to character attribution, in which adults attribute to the child such positive characteristics as generosity, helpfulness, and kindness. Although we do not understand fully the processes by which character attribution has an impact on behavior, it appears to have a somewhat different function for the child than rewards or demands for such behaviors. Attributions are attempts to modify the child's *image* of himself or herself in the direction of social competence. Telling a child that he or she *is* a very cooperative person, a careful worker, considerate, persistent in the face of frustration, and a conscientious student is designed to induce the child to think of himself or herself as such a person and behave accordingly. Although research on this behavior modification technique is relatively new, documentation of the efficacy of character attribution is impressive. As children become aware of themselves as unique individuals (displaying a composite of characteristics unlike those of any other individual) they seem to "take ownership" of their identity, investing in it, striving to maintain it, and taking pride in it. Positive attributions (brave, smart, kind) are flattering and presumably are willingly incorporated into the self-image of the child. To the extent that the child understands the message and can match behaviors to the attribution, one would expect the child to be motivated to perform in accord with it.

Radke-Yarrow and her colleagues caution the reader that attributions must be "believable" to the child to be incorporated into the concept of self. Although the point is well taken, children do appear to be persuaded by positive character attributions even when they are not necessarily based on objective fact. In a study by Jensen and Moore (1977), for example, school-age boys were randomly assigned to a cooperative or a competitive attribution condition prior to their participation in a block-building task with a peer. Children who were told that they were known to be "good cooperators" behaved cooperatively in the game, while those told they were known to be "good competitors" displayed significantly more competition with their partner. Apparently both attributions were sufficiently believable and salient as to predispose children to behave in accord with them even though the children were randomly assigned to the attribution conditions. Other investigators have confirmed the efficacy of positive attributions in eliciting charitable behavior (Grusec, Kuczynski, Rushton, & Simutis, 1978) and neatness (Miller, Brickman, & Bolen, 1975).

Both positive and negative character attributions are used by adults in their interactions with children throughout childhood, perhaps from age 2 on; children are told that they are big boys or girls, a good friend, a generous or kind person, naughty, stupid, or irresponsible. Negative attributions are offered in hopes that a child will find the characteristic unflattering enough to motivate change. Ironically, negative attributions may cause conflict in the child. The attribution is undesirable, to be sure, but the child's investment in preserving what is "me" may nevertheless have high valence for the child, causing the child to choose between changing and simply claiming ownership of the attribution and taking the consequences.

Character attributions probably should be used carefully by adults attempting to modify children's behavior. Although we know very little about the long-term impact of such manipulations, positive attributions appear to have a powerful impact on behavior. If used thoughtlessly, they could mislead children regarding their characteristics or abilities, or distress and confuse them if they do not actually possess the skills or insights to implement a flattering attribution that they believe — or wish to believe. Negative attributions should also be used with care inasmuch as they can be ego-damaging and discouraging to children. Also, negative attributions may be incorporated into the self-image without changing behavior. Smith and Geoffrey (1968) studied role attribution ("class clown," "lazy worker") in a school setting over a period of a year. It was clear from their observations that both teachers and peers helped to maintain positive and negative roles played by some of the children in a group through subtle attention and attribution.

Before leaving the topic of adult-child relations, a word should be said about the recent awareness among researchers of the extent to which children modify the behavior of adults interacting with them, just as adults socialize children. Sensitive parents respect individual differences in their offspring. They try to accommodate their children's special needs and desires and learn from their children what seems to be best for them. Children do their part by directly reinforcing their parents and other adults with smiles and approval for "acceptable" behavior and by protesting and fussing about acts and decisions that cause resentment.

The behavior of teachers too is undoubtedly modified by the successes and failures they experience as a consequence of their classroom interactions and decisions. Teachers would do well to consider what marks they would get from their students if they were to be graded by them on such things as sensitivity, consideration for others, fairness, and good company. Despite the absence of formal evaluation, teachers get constant feedback from their students that, if heeded, could enhance the teacher-child relationship, making sources of classroom influence reciprocal rather than unidirectional — teachers influence children, but children also influence teachers.

Attention now will be given to a discussion of each of the two social roles the child must master upon entering the elementary school, the role of *group member* and the role of *student*. Consideration will be given to the relevant skills and competencies of 5-year-olds to meet the demands of the kindergarten and to the role of the teacher in facilitating that adaptation.

THE ROLE OF PEER GROUP MEMBER

It is generally recognized by educators and others that the school's primary responsibility is to teach the child the academic skills of reading, writing, and math concepts and to prepare the child to be an informed, effective problem solver both in and out of the school context. Of critical importance to this latter goal is the extent to which the child learns to function as a productive member of the peer group. Piaget spoke of the preschool child's egocentrism — the fact that the child comes to the peer group with limited ability to take the perspective of another and hence to function as a member in a society of equals. The peer group in Piaget's scheme of things plays a significant role in intellectual and social development by exposing the child to egalitarian relationships for the first time. The early years of the child's life are dominated by the nonegalitarian relationships of the family, whose members are either older and more competent than the child or younger (as in the case of an infant or toddler sibling) and less competent. Even in the most democratic families, hierarchies of power and dominance are set by age and developmental competence, not by consensus or negotiation.

Despite limited experience in egalitarian social relationships, 5-year-olds bring to the kindergarten classroom a surprisingly sophisticated social repertoire. Observational studies carried out in early childhood settings such as nursery school, day care centers, and Head Start classrooms indicate that children not only display a plethora of positive social behaviors as they interact freely with each other but are active agents in the socialization of their fellow group members (Hartup, 1983; Moore, 1982; Rubin & Everett, 1982).

Friends and Acquaintances

What social skills do 5-year-olds bring to the peer group? Throughout the preschool years young children interacting in groups clearly are biased toward positive social exchanges with companions. In observations of nursery school and day care children at play, positive social interactions (friendly approaches, sharing, joining, initiating a conversation) outnumber negative, agonistic behaviors by ratios ranging from 3 : 1 to 7 : 1 or 8 : 1 (Moore, 1982).

Five-year-olds are socially skilled at approaching and initiating social contact with both familiar and unfamiliar peers, can enter an already established play group by asking to join or by discreetly blending into the group without disrupting its ongoing activities, and can generate reasonably sophisticated strategies for getting along with companions (Asher, Renshaw, & Hymel, 1982; Spivack & Shure, 1974). Although truly intimate relations, in which children share their innermost secrets and concerns with chosen friends, are common in middle childhood (Hartup, 1983), 5-year-olds are just beginning to show signs of intimacy by concentrating their attention on a small number of particular friends whom they seek out, share activities with, and support and defend as best they can. As is true with older children, 5-year-old girls appear to have a somewhat smaller but more intimate network of friends than boys whose friendship circles are more expansive and not as exclusionary. Both sexes, however, are learning how to acquire and maintain friends.

As children become friends, their social interactions increase in complexity. They verbalize to each other more, smile and laugh more, and display more affection for each other than for acquaintances (Doyle, 1982; Schwartz, 1972). In fact, cooperative activities appear to have bidirectional significance for the bonding of children throughout childhood in that children who are already friends seem able to perform cooperative tasks better than those who are not, but having cooperated on a task also biases children toward mutual friendly interactions that did not exist previous to their cooperative participation (DeVries & Edwards, 1973; Johnson & Johnson, 1975; Stendler, Damrin, & Haines, 1951).

During the past 10 to 15 years, cooperative learning strategies have been incorporated into many school programs. Children in these programs spend some part of their school day working toward shared educational goals or products. They may study together in small groups, tutor each other, or work independently on a segment of a product that eventually becomes part of a whole. Rewards for individual children are often (although not always) based on the final product or group success. Reviews of research on cooperative learning indicate that such learning environments facilitate individual as well as group learning, improve attitudes toward school, increase self-esteem of student participants, and increase interpersonal helping, concern about peers, and preference for working with peers (Johnson & Johnson, 1975; Sharan, 1980; Slavin, 1980). Although this work has been carried out with children older than 5, one would suspect that cooperative classroom activities would have many of the same advantages for the younger children.

Despite the relative immaturity of the young child, the period from 4 to 5 is a time when children are making great strides in understanding that other people have points of view that may differ from their own and that to function effectively with them one must take into account their feelings, their perceptions of events, and the consequences of events for others as well as for oneself. Contrary to this view of the competent young child, Piaget hypothesized that children as young as 5 not only were incapable of taking the perspective of another but also assumed that others shared their perspective (Piaget, 1965). Recently, however, investigators working in this domain of development have demonstrated that 5-year-olds not only can interpret accurately the emotional feelings of another from facial expressions and circumstantial evidence but can make appropriate inferences about another's needs based on that information, provided the child is familiar with the conditions about which he or she is making inferences (Shantz, 1975). Given this evidence, one might expect children to be particularly astute at judging the perspectives and intentions of companions about their own age who share a classroom and who have needs and motives that resemble their own — including having occasional moments of unmitigated selfishness and greed.

To be sure, 5-year-olds are better at imposing high behavioral standards on their companions than on themselves and are often torn between their own self-interest and what is obviously fair and reasonable, but they are not uninitiated at the time they enter the kindergarten. All have faced the dilemma of living with others who have needs and rights that must be observed, such as: One does not take things that belong to others, certain things are common belongings, the distribution of some valued resources is governed by equal shares, and one does not lie to escape blame or to victimize another. Five-year-olds should expect to have to abide by these standards at school as they do elsewhere.

Consideration for Others

Although young children are capable of empathic feelings and sympathetic acts at a very early age (Radke-Yarrow, Zahn-Waxler, & Chapman, 1983), they do not generally think of themselves as persons who provide supportive nurturance to others or who help others during a crisis. Young children are not at all inclined to place themselves in physical danger or suffer deprivation, fear, or anxiety in order to help another person — nor do we expect it of them. Despite the absence of overt instances of self-sacrifice and altruism, however, observations confirm that preschoolers are making steady progress on this aspect of social development (Moore, 1982). Giving support to others, in the form of affection and help, clearly is becoming a more prominent aspect of the child's social repertoire. Not only are help giving and nurturance giving on the increase relative to seeking, but children of 4 and 5 appear to be in transition as to the target of their seeking, with more of their seeking of both help and nurturance being addressed to peers rather than to adults. It seems that by 5, the children themselves recognize that their companions are capable of considering the needs of others and are casting their peers in the role of "giver" more often than occurred earlier in their development.

Adults would do well to foster this natural developmental transition from being primarily a seeker to balancing seeking and giving in peer group interactions, and from relying completely on adults for support to performing a support role for each other. Children need to be helped to think of themselves as fully capable of being kind and considerate of others. Teachers who have made a special effort to call the attention of their children to the needs of others and their role in helping have initiated classroom projects such as: Preparing an entertainment "care package" for a child who is ill and will be home for an extended time; sending a note of encouragement to a child who has moved to another school; making a hanging welcome sign for a new enrollee in the class; sending a greeting to a newborn sibling of a child in the group which includes drawings of what kindergarten is like, to be saved for the child; making a class phone call with a prepared list of questions to be asked of a member who is vacationing; sending a taped message to a family who lost their home in a tornado; and composing a poem honoring a person in their community who had received newspaper publicity for an act of bravery.

Children also can be helped to understand that their companions occasionally have difficult times and need their support — for example, when a grandparent dies or a pet is lost or killed. A child may wish to talk to the class about his or her feelings. The group may try to think of some ways to be especially kind to that child for a few days.

Young children do not typically think of such things on their own. They do respond to the challenge of helping others when opportunities present themselves, however, especially when an activity is a shared one that makes them feel competent and important. Children should be encouraged to relate their experiences to family members so they too can reinforce altruistic behavior in the children. Young children are not ready for genuinely sacrificial acts; school projects of these kinds should not require too much of the children or arouse their concerns about their ability to be helpful. In general, however, such events can be expected to provide the class with a moment of high *esprit de corps* that can be a valuable asset to the teacher and the school that is well worth the time and effort.

Conflict in the Classroom

Toward the end of the preschool period, children also are handling conflict and aggression in the peer group with surprising aplomb and sophistication (Hartup, 1983; Moore, 1982). The physical aggression that characterized the younger preschooler is gradually giving way to argument — especially by girls, but by boys as well in settings in which physical aggression is deemed inappropriate (such as during structured classroom activities). The aggression of older preschoolers, compared with younger ones, is less likely to be unprovoked and is more often retaliatory; hence it serves the useful social function of informing the aggressor of his or her indiscretion. Observations of nursery school children suggest that 5-year-olds are quite successful at discouraging the unwarranted agonistic behavior of their companions by expressing their displeasure, resisting unreasonable demands, and expecting fair treatment from peers (Patterson, Littman, & Bricker, 1967). In this regard, arguments of the older preschoolers are more often accompanied by rule quoting, reasoned justification of one's position, persuasion, compromise, and negotiation, compared with the fights of younger children. All of these techniques presumably force children to take into account the perspective of others as well as their own, moving them on from an egocentric to a sociocentric perspective.

In the kindergarten classroom children are likely to experience a more formal, institutionalized approach to misbehavior than that which characterized the preschool or neighborhood play group. Explicit rules will be made that govern interpersonal relations such as sharing, taking other people's things, cheating, being late, and disrupting classroom activities. Even dominance hierarchies among children are likely to be managed by, for example, implementing a system of turns for being first in line, distributing supplies, answering questions, and so on. Although there is no clear evidence of the ability of children of kindergarten age to participate in rule-making negotiations on their own behalf, one would suspect that they are capable of talking with their teacher about such issues and considering the need for rules to which all members must subscribe. One might expect more forgetting (if not more outright defiance) from younger children than from older children, but 5-year-olds appear to be ready to take this kind of responsibility under the guidance of their teacher (Spivack & Shure, 1974).

Teachers vary in how much responsibility they take for settling arguments and negotiating solutions to conflicts with the children in their classrooms. Five-year-old children are surprisingly capable of negotiating fair solutions on their own if given the time and freedom to do so. If children are allowed some latitude to express their anger and disapproval over a companion's unacceptable behavior, the message is likely to get across to the culprit. Pairs of children or small groups that frequently argue or take issue with each other can be asked to go off by themselves or with an adult to thrash out what they think happens between them that causes constant trouble. They may then be asked to report to the teacher about how they plan to manage their relationships in the future.

Social Status in the Peer Group

It is reassuring to know that children as young as 4 and 5 make judgments that resemble those of adults in assessing the social competencies of their peers. Measures of sociometric status indicate that children who are "popular" in the preschool and kindergarten peer group are more likely than unpopular children to be friendly and cooperative, enthusiastic about school activities, compliant with adults, and willing to observe the general social protocol of the classroom (Moore, 1982). Although moderate levels of appropriate aggression appear not to interfere with popularity, highly aggressive or disruptive children are not popular in the peer group. Children who display such behaviors typically get significantly more than their share of negative sociometric votes, as do children whose behavior is viewed as "bizarre" or "weird." Since popular children enjoy more social influence in the peer society than unpopular ones, they provide excellent role models for others and are a source of information on social protocol from which the less skillful children can learn. It is important to point out, however, that children who enjoy high status with peers are not clones of adult authority figures. They may, in fact, occasionally overstep the bounds of compliance expected by adults, press the limits of classroom protocol to the delight of other children, and occasionally dominate other children to the point of exploitation. Teachers need to help popular children learn to be fair and considerate despite the fact that they may be shielded from peer criticism by their popularity. Fortunately, popular children tend also to be socially sensitive and are likely to adapt their behavior accordingly when given appropriate feedback.

Unfortunately, socially immature and withdrawn children are in some danger of being overlooked by both peers and teachers in the classroom, since they do not have the positive impact on others that the popular child has or the negative impact that aggressive, disruptive children have. These children typically are neglected on sociometric measures as well, receiving neither positive nor negative nominations. Despite their low profile, children whose shyness, timidity, or immaturity is within the normal range of development appear to make quite adequate adjustments to the classroom. Northway (1944), in discussing these children, suggests that the child's own feeling of satisfaction with his or her degree of social involvement should be an important criterion for adults to use in deciding whether or not to worry about such a child. A child who is capable of making appropriate social overtures and having friendly exchanges with others but prefers a somewhat "laid-back" social style need not be cause for concern. On the other hand, a child who is obviously socially awkward or anxious and unhappy with his or her social involvement needs attention and help from teachers and peers.

Adults can sometimes talk confidentially with a child who is having trouble getting along with peers, seeking to understand the child's point of view and offering helpful suggestions. More progress can be made with difficult children if the child feels that the adult is truly trying to help so that the child will be more accepted and successful at school. If the circumstances are right, a teacher may wish to talk with the entire class about the problems of a difficult child (with the child's consent) so that they too can make helpful suggestions — and agree to be patient while the child is learning. Discussions of this kind need to be carefully controlled by the adults, however, so they do not turn into common gripe sessions.

THE ROLE OF STUDENT IN THE KINDERGARTEN

Young children come to school with predispositions and attitudes about learning that affect their adaptation to the role of student. Even children who have attended preschools or have been in center care during their early years seem to think of the elementary school as a milestone in their lives and the beginning of the "big stuff" — the time when one begins to read books and get homework. Inasmuch as attitudes and perceptions about school, and about the self as a student, appear to have a significant impact on achievement motivation and performance, it will serve as well to consider some of the psychological processes that have been under investigation by researchers during the past decade or more that are relevant to school adjustment.

Of particular importance for this discussion is the child's self-concept — especially academic self-concept, including the child's perception of the self as a learner with expectations regarding success and failure on academic tasks and a motivational orientation that is driven by a mixture of internal desire (to learn for the sake of learning itself, to master the content or skill) and external desire (a need to perform well to please a parent or teacher, obtain a good grade, or avoid negative feedback). Related to academic self-concept are constructs that reflect the child's understanding of the causes of achievement outcomes, which, in turn, lead to causal attributions about one's own academic successes and failures.

Although these processes have been studied primarily in school-age children and are most central to the stages of development of children 7 and older, they do appear to have some relevance for younger children. In order to provide appropriate preparatory experiences for kindergarten children, we need to understand as best we can the developmental milestones and hurdles that are on the horizon for them.

The Concept of the Self as Student

What do we know about these psychological phenomena in children at about the time they enter kindergarten? A capsule picture, glossing over individual differences in temperament, ability, and previous experience, would suggest that the typical kindergartener comes to school with the high expectation that it will be a positive experience, albeit with some apprehension about its newness. Compared with older children, young children have high self-esteem regarding their intellectual capabilities. For example, when asked to assess themselves, many more kindergarteners and first graders ranked themselves "near the top of their class" than there could possibly be, while second graders and beyond ranked themselves more objectively, as their teachers might (Harter, 1983; Nicholls, 1979). Also, younger children judge tasks to be "easier" than older children do and have higher expectancies of success. In her studies of children in grades 3 through 6, Harter (1983) reported a steady increase in the correlation between the child's *perceived* cognitive competence and *actual* competence, suggesting that children get progressively more accurate in assessing their cognitive abilities. By about 8 years of age, children begin to see themselves somewhat more modestly as "partly dumb" and "partly smart."

For the young child, self-esteem appears to be an outgrowth of other people's perceptions and the extent to which the child is made to feel good about himself or herself by significant others such as parents and teachers. In discussing this issue, Markus and her colleague make the point that the concept of self is a social phenomenon for all children (Markus & Nurius, 1984). Clearly, however, the older child also uses objective criteria against which to compare his or her achievements, whereas the young child lacks both the normative information for that task and the evaluation strategies to make the comparisons.

In the view of investigators studying cognitive development, it appears that children have made substantial progress in the ability to make social comparisons and evaluate themselves by age 7 or 8. Ironically, shortly after that time (about 9 or 10 years of age) a substantial drop in self-esteem has been observed, perhaps because of the child's developing ability to be self-critical. The younger child's naiveté with regard to self-evaluation and self-criticism may actually protect the child from becoming overly discouraged or demoralized by early ineptness in academic tasks.

Locus of Control and Attribution

Two additional psychological/cognitive constructs related to mastery motivation that have been studied extensively in the past 10 to 20 years are locus of control (Rotter, 1966) and attribution (Weiner & Kukla, 1970). *Locus of control* refers to the belief system of an individual with regard to causes of events, especially the causes of successes and failures in achievement-related situations. *Attribution* refers to the process of ascribing specific causes to the *self* or to *outside influences*. Locus of control may be viewed as *internal*, residing in the individual and under control of the individual, or *external*, beyond the control of the individual, leaving the individual relatively powerless to affect outcomes. Presumably school-age children with an internal orientation have a higher interest in mastery motivation for its own sake than externally oriented children and are more active and self-directed in dealing with novel or ambiguous achievement-related events. Externally oriented children, on the other hand, are motivated more by judgments of teachers and other powerful individuals who evaluate their achievements. Dweck and Elliott (1983) suggest a similar dichotomy in discussing children's choices of academic goals; internally oriented children favor "learning goals," in which achievement is its own reward, and externally oriented children favor "performance goals," in which displaying competence to others is uppermost.

Data on locus of control in preschoolers indicate that young children generally come to school with an *internal* orientation, expressing considerable confidence in their ability to control outcomes in achievement situations (Mischel, Zeiss, & Zeiss, 1974; Nowicki & Duke, 1974). These findings, combined with information from tests administered to older children, suggest that the relation between locus of control and age may be curvilinear, with the youngest children tested (preschoolers, kindergarteners, and first graders) and older children (junior high school age) maintaining an *internal* orientation while middle-childhood children maintain an *external* orientation.

Documenting the changes from an essentially internal motivational system to an external one as children are introduced to school tempts one to make the elementary school the "whipping boy" for taking the fun out of intellectual pursuits. It is well to keep in mind, however, that normal developmental/cognitive processes also contribute to making the young school-age child more externally oriented in achievement motivation. During this time, children are dramatically increasing their understanding of cognitive processes and content. In middle childhood children will become competent at making social comparisons for the purpose of evaluating their own and others' performances. They seem to *want* to challenge and test themselves, and they know with greater precision when they have failed and when they have succeeded. They make more realistic judgments than they once did with regard to why they have failed (although they may at times reject the implications of failure for the sake of self-esteem). These new cognitive/evaluative skills draw children's attention to external, objective comparisons of their own ability with that of others. Satisfaction is the greatest when others agree that you have indeed accomplished something significant.

As important as an internal orientation is to achievement behavior throughout the life span, one would suspect that no child can adapt well to the school environment without at least a moderately external orientation and a sensitivity to evaluation by grades and teacher assessment. One would hope that the school would do its part to encourage a balance of both orientations by providing individualized curricular activities that give expression to intrinsically as well as extrinsically motivated achievement. John Goodlad (1983), in his discussion of education in our country, expressed grave concern over this issue inasmuch as school curriculum rarely requires, or even invites, creative thinking, autonomous problem solving, and intrinsically motivated scholarship in children.

The second psychological/cognitive process related to mastery motivation that has received attention from investigators in the past decade is attribution theory, the process of attributing causes to events and outcomes (Weiner, 1979; Weiner & Kukla, 1970). Attributions of causes for academic outcomes of success and failure are typically classified into four categories: *ability* and *effort* (considered to be internal causes of achievement outcomes) and *task difficulty* and *luck* (external causes of such outcomes). Causes are further classified as stable (ability and task difficulty) or unstable (effort and luck). Attributing one's successes to an internal, stable cause, such as ability, should lead to high self-esteem and academic worth. Attributing *failures* to these same factors should be accompanied by low self-esteem and academic worth.

Attributing failure to an external factor (such as luck) rather than to an internal factor (such as effort) can predispose a child to settle for a lower level of performance than the child's ability would dictate. Children who experience repeated failure and attribute that failure to stable internal factors such as ability have been described by Dweck (1975) as victims of "learned helplessness," a phenomenon in which the child concludes that nothing can be done about school failure. In discussing the shift from internal to external attributions, Harter (1981) expresses concern that for some children the shift is accompanied by an exaggerated fear of failure, a reduced preference for challenge, an increased preference for easy tasks, greater dependence on teachers for guidance in mastery situations, and concern about grade getting as an end in itself. Harter makes the important point that school children should be rewarded for *effort*, not just *success*, in order to maintain a high level of motivation for academic challenge. The point is well taken; children who feel that "not to succeed is to fail" will be sorely tempted to protect themselves from the anxiety of failure by avoiding difficult tasks. Rewards for *effort* even without success on such tasks should help children to maintain high *perceived* competence in the face of failure. On this point, Harter presents evidence that children with high perceived competence do, indeed, choose more difficult tasks than those with low perceived competence. In fact, perceived competence predicted choice of difficult tasks better than actual competence, suggesting that attitudes and beliefs about academic failure are clearly involved in these task choices.

Despite some criticism of locus of control and attribution measures, research using these tests with adults and school-age children has been moderately successful in identifying children who differ significantly in achievement motivation and behavior. Research with children as young as 5 has been less successful. Children that young do not appear to understand abstract cause-and-effect relations, nor do they understand complex concepts such as "ability" and "luck." Evidence suggests that young children recognize specific abilities in themselves, such as the ability to ride a trike, tie shoes, or identify letters, but they do not yet understand the more stable concept of "ability" that transcends time and task. Cognitive maturation and school experience will lead them closer to these insights within a year or two. In the meantime, children of kindergarten age are capable of becoming extremely anxious and upset in situations in which they fear not being able to manage tasks. Experiences that cause school to have a negative valence for the 5-year-old may pave the way for counterproductive self-protective attributions in achievement situations a few years down the road.

The "back-to-basics" movement in education is having its effect on curricula in school districts all over our country. In many kindergarten classrooms children are expected to acquire academic skills that formerly were part of the first-grade curriculum. Criteria for mastery are more stringent, and the phenomenon of "flunking" kindergarten is a reality for many children and their families. Whether the new academic goals for 5-year-old children are appropriate or not is important, of course, but irrelevant to the topic of this chapter. The impact of early failure on children's self-esteem and motivation as students is relevant, however. It is difficult to imagine that early-grade failure in school could be a constructive experience, for more than a handful of 5-year-old children, causing them to apply themselves and hence succeed in their own eyes and in the eyes of their teachers and parents. For many children, early failure will have a depressive effect on both self-confidence and motivation, dampening the child's enthusiasm for the learning process in general and for school in particular. Remedial education strategies, including holding children back a grade, should be managed in ways that preserve children's self-esteem and enthusiasm for school.

Summary Comments

Kindergarten teachers have a unique role in the lives of children; they are the ones who introduce children to school and send them on their way into the elementary grades. Children typically come to the kindergarten classroom with high anticipation and enthusiasm — a little wary perhaps, but generally confident, motivated to learn for learning's sake, and eager to please their teachers and live amicably with their peers. Among the goals of the kindergarten program is to help children feel good about themselves as students and about school as a place to learn in the company of peers. Children of kindergarten age are still very dependent on adults for feedback as to how well they are doing. They need to be taught to recognize and appreciate their academic successes but also to tolerate their failures. Five-year-olds do not need to be shielded completely from frustration and failure; they are capable of getting the message that hard work is called for and that they are expected to do the best they can. To have a child complete an entire year of school without ever having been challenged by the experience of falling short of a goal set for the child is to deprive the child of the satisfaction of measuring up to a challenge — of taking pride in surmounting a difficult task by trying again and succeeding. Children who are not giving school their best shot need to have more expected of them. Along the way, failure must be "defused" as a source of debilitating anxiety. The child will be well served by a nurturant, supportive teacher who helps keep things in perspective, who lets the child know that all of us fail from time to time, and who structures the learning tasks so that the vision of success is close enough at hand to be within the short purview of the child. The children will do the rest.

REFERENCES

Asher, S. R., Renshaw, P. D., & Hymel, S. (1982). Peer relations and the development of social skills. In S. G. Moore & C. R. Cooper, (Eds.), *The young child: Reviews of research: Vol. 3* (pp. 137–158). Washington, DC: National Association for the Education of Young Children.

Baldwin, A. L. (1948). Socialization and the parent-child relationship. *Child Development, 19,* 127–136.

Baumrind, D. (1971). Current patterns of parental authority. *Developmental Psychology Monograph, 4,* 1–103.

Becker, W. C. (1964). Consequences of parental discipline. In M. L. Hoffman & L. W. Hoffman (Eds.), *Review of child development research: Vol. 1* (pp. 169–208). New York: Russell Sage Foundation.

The Consortium for Longitudinal Studies. (1983). *As the twig is bent: Lasting effects of preschool programs.* Hillsdale, NJ: Erlbaum.

DeVries, D. L., & Edwards, K. J. (1973). Learning games and student teams: Their effects on classroom process. *American Educational Research Journal, 10,* 307–318.

Doyle, A. (1982). Friends, acquaintances, and strangers: The influence of familiarity and ethnolinguistic background on social interaction. In K. H. Rubin

& H. S. Ross, (Eds.), *Peer relationships and social skills in childhood* (pp. 229–252). New York: Springer-Verlag.

Dweck, C. S. (1975). The role of expectations and attributions in the alleviation of learned helplessness. *Journal of Personality and Social Psychology, 31,* 674–685.

Dweck, C. S., & Elliott, E. S. (1983). Achievement motivation. In P. H. Mussen & E. M. Hetherington (Eds.), *Handbook of child psychology: Vol. 4. Socialization, personality, and social development* (pp. 643–691) New York: Wiley.

Goodlad, J. (1983). Individuality, commonality, and curricular practice. In G. Fenstermacher & J. Goodlad (Eds.), *Individual differences and the common curriculum.* Eighty-second Yearbook of the National Society for the Study of Education, Part 1. Chicago: University of Chicago Press.

Grusec, J. E., Kuczynski, L., Rushton, J. P., & Simutis, Z. (1978). Modeling, direct instruction, and attributions: Effects on altruism. *Developmental Psychology, 14,* 51–57.

Harris, F. R., Wolf, M. M., & Baer, D. M. (1967). Effects of adult social reinforcement on child behavior. In W. W. Hartup & N. L. Smothergill (Eds.), *The young child* (pp. 13–26). Washington, DC: National Association for the Education of Young Children.

Harter, S. (1981). A model of mastery motivation in children: Individual differences and developmental change. In W. A. Collins (Ed.), *Minnesota Symposia on Child Psychology: Vol. 14. Aspects of the development of competence* (pp. 215–225). Hillsdale, NJ: Erlbaum.

Harter, S. (1983). Developmental perspective on the self system. In P. H. Mussen & E. M. Hetherington (Eds.), *Handbook of child psychology: Vol. 4. Socialization, personality, and social development* (pp. 275–385). New York: Wiley.

Hartup, W. E. (1983). Peer relations. In P. H. Mussen & E. M. Hetherington (Volume Eds.), P. H. Mussen (Series Ed.), *Handbook of child psychology: Vol. 4. Socialization, personality, and social development* (pp. 103–196). New York: Wiley.

Hoffman, M. L. (1963). Parent discipline and the child's consideration for others. *Child Development, 34,* 573–588.

Jensen, R. E., & Moore, S. G. (1977). The effect of attribution statements on cooperativeness and competitiveness in school-age boys. *Child Development, 48,* 305–307.

Johnson, D. W., & Johnson, R. T. (1975). *Learning together and alone.* Englewood Cliffs, NJ: Prentice-Hall.

Kagan, J., & Moss, H. A. (1962). *Birth to maturity.* New York: Wiley.

Lepper, M. R., Greene, D., & Nisbett, R. E. (1973). Undermining children's intrinsic interest with extrinsic rewards: A test of the "over-justification" hypothesis. *Journal of Personality and Social Psychology, 28,* 129–137.

Maccoby, E. E., & Martin, J. A. (1983). Socialization in the context of the family: Parent-child interaction. In P. H. Mussen & E. M. Hetherington (Eds.), *Handbook of child psychology: Vol. 4. Socialization, personality, and social development* (pp. 1–101). New York: Wiley.

Markus, H. J., & Nurius, P. S. (1984). Self-understanding and self-reputation in middle childhood. In W. A. Collins (Ed.), *Development during middle childhood* (pp. 147–183). Washington, DC: National Academic Press.

Miller, R. L., Brickman, P., & Bolen, D. (1975). Attribution versus persuasion as a means for modifying behavior. *Journal of Personality and Social Psychology, 31*, 430–441.

Mischel, W., Zeiss, R., & Zeiss, A. (1974). Internal-external control and persistence: Validation and implications of the Stanford Preschool Internal-External Scale. *Journal of Personality and Social Psychology, 29*, 265–278.

Moore, S. G. (1982). Prosocial behavior in the early years: Parent and peer influences. In B. Spodek (Ed.), *Handbook of research in early childhood education* (pp. 65–81). New York: Free Press.

Nicholls, J. G. (1979). Quality and equality in intellectual development: The role of motivation in education. *American Psychologist, 34*, 1071–1084.

Northway, M. (1944). Outsiders: A study of personality patterns in children least acceptable to their age mates. *Sociometry, 7*, 10–25.

Nowicki, S., & Duke, M. P. (1974). A preschool and primary internal-external control scale. *Developmental Psychology, 10*, 874–880.

Patterson, G. R., Littman, R. A., & Bricker, W. (1967). Assertive behavior in children: A step toward a theory of aggressiveness. *Monographs of the Society for Research in Child Development, 32*, (113).

Piaget, J. (1965). *The moral judgment of the child*. New York: Free Press.

Radke-Yarrow, M., Zahn-Waxler, C., & Chapman, M. (1983). Children's prosocial dispositions and behavior. In P. H. Mussen & E. M. Hetherington (Eds.), *Handbook of child psychology: Vol. 4. Socialization, personality, and social development* (pp. 469–545). New York: Wiley.

Rosenhan, D. (1969). Some origins of concern for others. In P. Mussen, J. Langer, & M. Covington (Eds.), *Trends and issues in developmental psychology* (pp. 134–153). New York: Holt, Rinehart and Winston.

Rosenthal, R., & Jacobson, L. (1968). *Pygmalion in the classroom*. New York: Holt, Rinehart and Winston.

Rotter, J. B. (1966). Generalized expectancies for internal vs. external control of reinforcement. *Psychology Monographs, 80*, 1–28.

Rubin, K. H., & Everett, B. (1982). Social perspective-taking in young children. In S. G. Moore & C. R. Cooper (Eds.), *The young child: Reviews of research, Vol. 3* (pp. 97–113). Washington, DC: National Association for the Education of Young Children.

Sears, R. R., Maccoby, E. E., & Levin, H. (1957). *Patterns of child rearing*. Evanston, IL: Row, Peterson and Co.

Schwartz, J. C. (1972). Effects of peer familiarity on the behavior of preschoolers in a novel situation. *Journal of Personality and Social Psychology, 24*, 276–284.

Shantz, C. V. (1975). *The development of social cognition*. Chicago: University of Chicago Press.

Sharan, S. (1980). Cooperative learning in small groups: Recent methods and effects on achievement attitudes, and ethnic relations. *Review of Educational Research, 50*, 241–271.

Slavin, R. E. (1980). Cooperative learning. *Review of Educational Research, 50,* 315–342.

Smith, L., & Geoffrey, W. (1968). *Complexities of an urban classroom.* New York: Holt, Rinehart and Winston.

Spivack, G., & Shure, M. B. (1974). *Social adjustment of young children.* San Francisco: Jossey-Bass.

Stendler, C. B., Damrin, D., & Haines, A. C. (1951). Studies in cooperation and competition: I. The effects of working for group and individual rewards on the social climate of children's groups. *Journal of Genetic Psychology, 79,* 173–198.

Weikart, D. P. (1983). A longitudinal view of a preschool research effort. In M. Perlmutter (Ed.), *The Minnesota Symposia on Child Psychology: Vol. 16. Developmental and policy concerning children with special needs.*

Weiner, B. (1979). A theory of motivation for some classroom experiences. *Journal of Educational Psychology, 71,* 3–25.

Weiner, B., & Kukla, A. (1970). An attributional analysis of achievement motivation. *Journal of Personality and Social Psychology, 15,* 1–20.

Yarrow, L. J., Rubenstein, J. L., & Pederson, F. A. (1972). Dimensions of early stimulation: Differential effects on infant development. *Merrill-Palmer Quarterly, 18,* 205–218.

CHAPTER 8

Using the Knowledge Base

Bernard Spodek

There have been serious debates in the United States about what kin-dergarten education should be. Some early childhood educators have argued that kindergarten programs have served young children well over the past generations and that these programs should be left alone. Other educators have argued that traditional kindergarten programs are anti-quated and inadequate. The knowledge provided in this book can help educators and policymakers address issues related to the nature of the kindergarten. It can inform decisions being made about kindergarten education as well as educational practice. Suggestions for areas of research that need to be addressed can also be generated from this material.

INFORMING PUBLIC POLICY AND PRACTICE

Perhaps the most effective way to use this volume is to address some of the myths that are believed regarding kindergarten education. Myths are traditional forms of knowledge that are used to explain phenomena. Myths about kindergarten may derive from research; some research find-ings are overgeneralized. Other myths are abstracted from the experience of practitioners. Still other myths evolve from strongly held values regard-ing children, families, and schools. Following is a selection of myths about kindergarten education.

Myths About Kindergarten

MYTH: Because so many pressures are placed on young children today, the nature of childhood is being eroded. We need to pro-tect these children by creating a pressure-free, conflict-free set-ting in kindergarten, one that makes as few demands on young children as possible.

There is no doubt that children are faced with a great many pressures as they grow up in our society. But rather than attempt to roll back history or create a protected paradise for some part of each child's day, we need to help children cope with the pressures they encounter. Early childhood programs should be challenging without being frustrating to children. They must be consistent with our social values while being developmentally appropriate. They should anticipate what will be expected of children in the future while, at the same time, being relevant to children's current lives.

We need to accept and cannot hide from the realities of growing up today in America. In accepting this, we need to create programs that are both stimulating to children and are supportive of children.

> MYTH: Young children today know more and have greater and more varied experiences than their counterparts of generations past. Therefore, they are capable of learning a great deal more than what was expected in the past.

There seem to be some trade-offs on how children are developing knowledge today. While they appear to know more, young children's developing learning and thinking styles may make it more difficult for us to educate them in traditional topics using conventional means. They may also have difficulty in applying what they have learned out of school to school tasks.

Changing community and family patterns have led to more fragmented families in America today. In addition, more children are being born to teenagers out of wedlock, and more children with medical problems are surviving birth and infancy. This has led to a wider range of individual differences among children in kindergarten, many of whom are difficult to educate. Added to this range of individual differences is the variety of language and cultural heritages from which kindergarten children come. Rather than make generalizations about what 5-year-olds can and cannot do, we need to discover the strengths and needs of each individual child coming to school.

> MYTH: If schools would concentrate on teaching the basics and nothing else, we would better prepare our children for success in future schooling and in the real world.

A person must be literate to survive in today's world, but people must know much more than how to read. We expect American citizens to participate in the political process. Being involved in making choices requires being aware of political issues, economic issues, and environmental issues, to name but a few significant areas.

While schools must be concerned with the requirements of future occupational and civic responsibilities, they must also be concerned with the quality of life as experienced in the present and in the future. Children's self-knowledge and an understanding and appreciation of the aesthetic elements of life all contribute to that quality.

> MYTH: Once children learn the relationship between written letters and spoken sounds, they can become competent readers.

Reading is more than sounding out words; it is gaining meaning from the printed page. This requires an understanding of a great many aspects of language along with a recognition of the relationship between letters and sounds. Knowledge of the meanings of words and phrases as well as awareness of the structure of the language and of the relationship of word meanings to their contexts are needed for children to move from reading symbols to reading ideas. A language-rich environment in which adults regularly use reading and writing, one that allows children to see the relationship between the two language systems and systematically introduces children to reading and writing, can help children develop an understanding of the reading process. Programs that limit reading activities to workbook tasks also limit children's opportunities to learn about language and reading.

> MYTH: If we can get children to verbalize a concept and repeat it often enough, they will come to learn and understand that concept.

Cognitive knowledge is created through intellectual activity. For young children the mental activity involved in concept development is accompanied by parallel physical activity. Research has helped us become aware that when we limit children's learning experiences to workbook-oriented kindergarten activities we limit what children can know. An active, inquiry-oriented program that requires children to adapt their understanding to their environment challenges children and leads them to become more knowledgeable and more competent intellectually.

> MYTH: Play is a frivolous activity without any serious consequences. It has no place in a kindergarten devoted to helping children learn those things that will prepare them for later schooling.

Research has shown that children engage in a variety of intellectual and social functions as they play with materials and with other children. Most important, children gather and process information through play. They learn to consider other people's points of view and develop ways to resolve both intellectual and social conflicts. In addition, they learn to understand and manipulate symbols as they use objects to represent something other than what they really are.

Teachers establish productive play settings and help children engage in educational play. They also intervene in children's play to help it better serve intellectual as well as social and creative functions. A range of play opportunities can be created in kindergarten which can serve to stimulate and integrate a wide range of children's learning.

MYTH: Since children have a great many opportunities to learn social skills at home, they can be ignored at school. Besides, the focus on intellectual rather than social skills ensures academic success.

Studies of intervention programs strongly suggest a link between children's social ability and academic success. We cannot separate the various realms of human development when we deal with children. The truism that the whole child comes to school needs to be understood and accepted with all of its ramifications. Thus, educators must be concerned with social learning and development even when giving priority to intellectual development and academic achievement.

Myths tend to be a familiar form of knowledge, and as such, they are comforting to those who hold them and are difficult to give up. Yet if we are to improve the education we provide kindergarten children we must assess what we believe to be true in relation to the best available knowledge.

We must also accept the fact that there are limits to our knowledge and that we must sometimes act beyond those limits as educators. Within these limits, however, we must use what we have come to know about children, families, society, and schools, to create the best education we can within our personal and professional limits. We must also use what we know to serve as a platform to search for greater knowledge.

SEEKING NEW KNOWLEDGE

One of the uses of the existing knowledge base of kindergarten education is to identify areas of needed research and to generate hypotheses to be tested in future study. As we look at our current knowledge base, it becomes evident that several areas of inquiry are worthy of further study at present.

Learning More About Children
Growing Up in America Today

Kindergartens must serve contemporary American society. They must relate to children as they exist today. We must continually discover and rediscover the conditions under which children are developing and the effects of those conditions on the children who attend our kindergartens.

Increasingly we are seeing young, single-parent families, families with only a single child, and "blended" families, where the children being raised are the result of more than one marriage. We are also seeing increasing numbers of families where both parents work. Indeed, the majority of mothers of kindergarten age are employed outside the home full-time. We need to study the consequences of these changing patterns on children who are growing up today. We also need to identify the services required to support the healthy development of these children. Extended-day kindergartens and child care services planned around school programs might need to be provided by schools or other agencies to avoid child neglect. New forms of communication with families might need to be established in order to maintain the ever-so-important home-school relations of the kindergarten.

We also need to inquire into the ways by which we can optimize learning and development in children with varied developmental patterns and different sets of strengths and needs. We need to seek better ways of matching our educational programs to the particular children being served by those programs. We need to increase our knowledge of children's social development, cognitive development, and language development. But we also need to learn more about the consequences on development and learning of what we do with children in kindergartens. We need to become increasingly aware of the relationship of teachers' actions on this learning. While we are learning a great deal at present about children's play and the consequences of this play, for example, there are few studies of teachers' play interventions and the consequences of play interventions on children's learning and activity patterns. Too often we read of recommendations for modification of kindergarten practice without serious study and reflection regarding the impact of these modifications on the children being served.

USING KNOWLEDGE WISELY AND JUSTLY

In exploring the knowledge base of kindergarten education, we have looked at what we know to be *true*. Kindergarten programs are also based on what we know to be *right*. It is our values that ultimately determine how we act, with scientific knowledge informing those actions. Let me suggest the following guidelines for actions related to kindergarten education:

Kindergartens Should Be Available to All Children

Kindergarten programs should not be limited to serving selected populations. Access should not be limited by ability to pay, nor should kindergarten education be denied to children who live in isolated or rural areas. We need to seek a range of delivery systems to provide access to kindergarten to all young children.

Kindergarten Programs Should Support Children's Developmental Needs

Kindergartens should be challenging, interesting, and pleasant places to be. They should be organized in terms of what young children are capable of knowing and doing. Kindergartens should be designed to help equalize the experiences of children of varying backgrounds. They should also serve to identify special problems in children and begin to provide appropriate services related to those problems.

Kindergartens Should Support Children's Individual Growth Patterns

Children are growing up in a society that is personally and culturally diverse. They differ in social, physical, emotional, and cognitive characteristics. These differences should be valued, and kindergarten programs should respond to and reflect the uniqueness of each child.

Kindergarten Should Be Taught by Qualified Individuals

Teaching young children requires special competencies and knowledge. Teachers who work with young children must have the basic understanding to make appropriate decisions and to respond to children in educationally meaningful ways. The differences between early childhood education and other levels of education should be recognized and valued.

Kindergarten Programs Should Provide
Bridges Within Children's Lives

Young children are influenced by many institutions. The kindergartens that they attend should seek ways to develop mutual trust between home and school. Kindergartens must also be aware of other institutions serving children and strive to coordinate services. Kindergartens should serve as effective bridges to programs that have served children before and will serve children after the kindergarten experience.

Within these guidelines we must strive to provide worthwhile educational experiences for young children. These experiences should be developmentally appropriate, and should lead to worthwhile educational outcomes. In addition, they should be consistent with the values of society and community. Only in meeting these guidelines will we serve young children well in kindergartens.

About the Editor and the Contributors

EUGENE E. GARCÍA is Director of the Center for Bilingual/Bicultural Education and Professor of Education in the College of Education at Arizona State University. He received his Ph.D. in Child Development from the University of Kansas and served as a Postdoctoral Fellow in Developmental Psycholinguistics at Harvard University in 1976, as a National Research Council Fellow in 1980, and currently is serving as a Kellogg National Fellow. He has published extensively in the areas of language acquisition, bilingual development, and the education of language minority students. His most recent edited volume is *Advances in Bilingual Education Research*.

CONSTANCE KAMII is Professor of Early Childhood Education at the University of Alabama at Birmingham. After receiving a Ph.D. from the University of Michigan in 1965, she collaborated with Jean Piaget in research at the International Center of Genetic Epistemology, and held a joint appointment with the University of Geneva and the University of Illinois at Chicago, 1973–83. Her research has focused on the application of Piaget's theory to early childhood education, and she is the author of *Physical Knowledge in Preschool Education, Number in Preschool and Kindergarten*, and *Young Children Reinvent Arithmetic*.

JANA M. MASON is Associate Professor of Educational Psychology at the University of Illinois at Urbana-Champaign. Her research has focused on early reading development and kindergarten reading instruction. She is the co-author of a textbook on reading instruction for elementary school teachers, *Reading Instruction for Today*, and a book on theoretical and instructional aspects of reading, *Reading Comprehension: Perspectives and Suggestions*. She is currently studying young children's changing understanding of reading and language from the preschool years through first grade.

SHIRLEY G. MOORE received her Ph.D. from the University of Iowa in 1960 and currently is Professor at the Institute of Child Development and Director of the Center for Early Education and Development at the University of Minnesota. She is co-author of *Contemporary Preschool Education* and co-editor of *Evaluation of Educational Programs for Young Children*. Dr. Moore has published research on aspects of preschool development including peer acceptance, communication factors affecting compliance with prohibitions, and curiosity.

OLIVIA N. SARACHO is Associate Professor at the University of Maryland. She completed her Ph.D. in early childhood education at the University of Illinois in 1978. Prior to that, she taught Head Start, preschool, kindergarten, and elementary classes in Brownsville, Texas, and was Director of the Child Development Associate Program at Pan American University. Her current research and writing are in the areas of cognitive style, academic learning, and teacher education in relation to early childhood education. Dr. Saracho is the co-author of *Foundations of Early Childhood Education*.

BERNARD SPODEK (editor) is Professor of Early Childhood Education at the University of Illinois, Urbana-Champaign, where he has taught since 1965. He received his doctoral degree from Teachers College, Columbia University, and has taught nursery school, kindergarten, elementary school, and college classes. Dr. Spodek has lectured extensively in the United States, Canada, China, England, Israel, Japan, Mexico, and Australia. He is widely published in the field of early childhood education. From 1976 through 1978, he was President of the National Association for the Education of Young Children, and from 1981 through 1983, he chaired the Early Education and Child Development Special Interest Group of the American Educational Research Association.

HERBERT ZIMILES is currently Senior Research Fellow and visiting Professor of psychology at the University of Michigan in Ann Arbor. Also a Senior Research Scientist in the Research Division of Bank Street College of Education in New York City, Dr. Zimiles has written extensively on educational evaluation and cognitive and personality development. He is co-author of *The Psychological Impact of School Experience* and co-editor of *Thought and Feeling: A Developmental Perspective*. Much of his recent writing, including a report to the National Commission on Excellence in Education, comes out of his current research on changing patterns of development in today's children.

INDEX

Index

Academic instruction in kindergarten, 5, 32
Achievement
early, power of, 5
expectations and, 117–118
Acquaintances in kindergarten,
122–124
Administration for Children,
Youth, and Families, 25
Adult-child interaction in kindergarten classroom, 111–121
attribution, 119–121
demands and expectations,
117–119
modeling and process of identification, 115–117
nurturance, 114–115
positive social reinforcement,
112–114
Age
and play materials, 102–103
and social play, 100
Age of Reason, education in,
40–41
Aggression in kindergarten
children, 125–126
All-day kindergarten, viii
Arenas, S., 25
Arguments among kindergarten
children, 125–126
Art
in kindergarten, 36
and literacy training, 59

Asher, S. R., 122
Asian Americans, 15, 17
Associative play, 93–94, 100
Attention span of children, 12
Attribution, character, 119–121
Attribution theory, 129,
131–132
Autonomy as educational aim,
84–86

Bakeman, R., 100
Barker, R. B., 102
Barnes, K. E., 100
Bates, E., 18
Baumrind, D., 117
Becker, W. C., 115
Behavior, childhood, changing
patterns of, 6–9
broadened span of child
population, 8–9
educability, 7
emotional stability, 7–8
organization and discipline, 6
social poise and self-assertiveness, 6
Berkeley, G., 67
Bibes, B., 2
Bible, 39, 40
Bilingual education, 24–29
effect on linguistic and cognitive development, 26–27
legislation, 25

DATE DUE
REMINDER

OCT 08 '99

MAY 0 1 2010

Please do not remove
this date due slip.